Gradle Recipes for Android

Master the New Build System for Android

Ken Kousen

T0219213

Beijing · Boston · Farnham · Sebastopol · Tokyo

Gradle Recipes for Android

by Ken Kousen

Copyright © 2016 Gradleware, Inc. All rights reserved.

Printed in the United States of America.

Published by O'Reilly Media, Inc., 1005 Gravenstein Highway North, Sebastopol, CA 95472.

O'Reilly books may be purchased for educational, business, or sales promotional use. Online editions are also available for most titles (*http://safaribooksonline.com*). For more information, contact our corporate/institutional sales department: 800-998-9938 or *corporate@oreilly.com*.

Editors: Heather Scherer and Brian Foster	**Indexer:** Angela Howard
Production Editor: Colleen Lobner	**Interior Designer:** David Futato
Copyeditor: Colleen Toporek	**Cover Designer:** Karen Montgomery
Proofreader: Kim Cofer	**Illustrator:** Rebecca Demarest

June 2016: First Edition

Revision History for the First Edition

2016-06-02: First Release

See *http://oreilly.com/catalog/errata.csp?isbn=9781491947029* for release details.

The O'Reilly logo is a registered trademark of O'Reilly Media, Inc. *Gradle Recipes for Android*, the cover image of a great potoo, and related trade dress are trademarks of O'Reilly Media, Inc.

While the publisher and the author have used good faith efforts to ensure that the information and instructions contained in this work are accurate, the publisher and the author disclaim all responsibility for errors or omissions, including without limitation responsibility for damages resulting from the use of or reliance on this work. Use of the information and instructions contained in this work is at your own risk. If any code samples or other technology this work contains or describes is subject to open source licenses or the intellectual property rights of others, it is your responsibility to ensure that your use thereof complies with such licenses and/or rights.

978-1-491-94702-9

[LSI]

This book is dedicated to my wife Ginger: my best friend, my partner, and the love of my life.

Twenty-five years is just the beginning.

Table of Contents

Foreword

This is the book we needed. We were about halfway through writing *Head First Android Development* when Google switched IDEs. At the time, pretty much everyone was using Eclipse with the Android Development Toolkit installed. But now, Google was pushing for developers to switch to the *Idea*-based *Android Studio*.

We're used to this kind of thing—most technical authors are. Some manufacturer startup switches from some new shiny thing to some even newer, even shinier thing. It happens all the time. You rewrite all your example code, update all the images, drop the features that are now irrelevant, and include what's most useful from the new technology. But what made the switch from Eclipse to Android Studio *different* was that under the hood the new IDE had a much, much more powerful engine.

Android Studio used Gradle for building, packaging, and deploying code. Other than knowing the name, neither of us had any experience of using Gradle directly. It was *kind of* like Maven, but rather than using lengthy XML configuration files, it used a sturdy and concise scripting language: Groovy.

We replaced all the screenshots, and updated the text in the seven or so chapters that were already written and then moved on to write the rest of the book. But it soon became clear that the process of creating applications with Gradle was subtly, but significantly different. Pretty much anything that you could do from the IDE was suddenly possible from the command line, which meant we could automate our build pipelines. It took just a few key presses to try out different library versions, or different build flavors. And because everything is just code, we could write the builds in the same way that we wrote the rest of the app.

Learning Gradle is now an important task for *every* Android developer. It's up there with knowing Java, or understanding the Activity lifecycle. But learning Gradle through trial-and-error can sometimes be a painful process. And that's where this book comes in. In these pages, you'll find a wealth of useful recipes that will help you avoid the commonest build problems. Whether you're setting up a testing system, automating your signed APK production, or just trying to speed up your build pipeline, this book is for you. Ken's lively writing style and realistic examples will keep you coming back again and again. With this book, Ken has shown that not only is he the go-to guy for Groovy, he's now also the go-to guy for Gradle.

—Dawn and David Griffiths
Authors, Head First
Android Development
April 20th, 2016

Preface

About the Book

This book contains recipes for working with the Gradle build system for Android projects. Gradle is one of the most popular tools for building applications from the Java world, and is expanding into other languages like C++. The Android team at Google adopted Gradle as the preferred build system for Android in the spring of 2013, and its use has grown steadily since then.

Since Gradle comes from the Groovy ecosystem, many Android developers may not be familiar with it. Groovy, however, is very easy for existing Java developers to learn. The purpose of this book is to provide examples that help you use Gradle to accomplish the most common build tasks for Android applications.

All code examples use Android SDK version 23, with emulators from either Marshmallow (Android 6) or Lollipop (Android 5.*). Android Studio versions 2.0 or 2.1 (beta) were used as the primary IDE, which included Gradle version 2.10 or above as the build tool.

Prerequisites

The Gradle plugin for Android involves at least some knowledge of Java, Groovy, Gradle, and Android. Since entire books are available for each of those topics, they can't all be covered in detail here.

The text in this book is aimed chiefly at developers who are comfortable with Android development. Very little Android background is provided, though complete code listings of all examples are available through the book's GitHub repository. Understanding Android means understanding Java, so that background is assumed as well.

Very little knowledge of either Groovy or Gradle is assumed, however. Appendix A contains a quick summary of Groovy syntax and techniques. Groovy concepts are also reviewed as they come up in various recipes. Appendix B has basic Gradle information, but the recipes themselves discuss Gradle in detail throughout the book.

Beyond those limitations, the book is designed to be as self-contained as possible, with links to external references (especially documentation) provided wherever appropriate.

The book also makes extensive use of Android Studio, as it is now the only officially supported IDE for Android development. Android Studio provides views and tools for Gradle, which are illustrated in many recipes. While the book is not designed to be a tutorial on Android Studio, its relevant features are shown wherever possible, and if that helps the reader learn more about the IDE, so much the better.

Conventions Used in This Book

The following typographical conventions are used in this book:

Italic
> Indicates new terms, URLs, email addresses, filenames, and file extensions.

`Constant width`
> Used for program listings, as well as within paragraphs to refer to program elements such as variable or function names, databases, data types, environment variables, statements, and keywords.

`Constant width bold`
> Shows commands or other text that should be typed literally by the user.

`Constant width italic`
> Shows text that should be replaced with user-supplied values or by values determined by context.

 This element signifies a tip or suggestion.

 This element signifies a general note.

This element indicates a warning or caution.

Using Code Examples

Supplemental material (code examples, exercises, etc.) is available for download at *https://github.com/kousen/GradleRecipesForAndroid*.

This book is here to help you get your job done. In general, if example code is offered with this book, you may use it in your programs and documentation. You do not need to contact us for permission unless you're reproducing a significant portion of the code. For example, writing a program that uses several chunks of code from this book does not require permission. Selling or distributing a CD-ROM of examples from O'Reilly books does require permission. Answering a question by citing this book and quoting example code does not require permission. Incorporating a significant amount of example code from this book into your product's documentation does require permission.

We appreciate, but do not require, attribution. An attribution usually includes the title, author, publisher, and ISBN. For example: "*Gradle Recipes for Android* by Ken Kousen (O'Reilly). Copyright 2016 Gradleware, Inc., 978-1-4919-4702-9."

If you feel your use of code examples falls outside fair use or the permission given above, feel free to contact us at *permissions@oreilly.com*.

Safari® Books Online

 *Safari Books Online* is an on-demand digital library that delivers expert content in both book and video form from the world's leading authors in technology and business.

Technology professionals, software developers, web designers, and business and creative professionals use Safari Books Online as their primary resource for research, problem solving, learning, and certification training.

Safari Books Online offers a range of plans and pricing for enterprise, government, education, and individuals.

Members have access to thousands of books, training videos, and prepublication manuscripts in one fully searchable database from publishers like O'Reilly Media, Prentice Hall Professional, Addison-Wesley Professional, Microsoft Press, Sams, Que, Peachpit Press, Focal Press, Cisco Press, John Wiley & Sons, Syngress, Morgan Kaufmann, IBM Redbooks, Packt, Adobe Press, FT Press, Apress, Manning, New Riders, McGraw-Hill, Jones & Bartlett, Course Technology, and hundreds more. For more information about Safari Books Online, please visit us online.

How to Contact Us

Please address comments and questions concerning this book to the publisher:

O'Reilly Media, Inc.
1005 Gravenstein Highway North
Sebastopol, CA 95472
800-998-9938 (in the United States or Canada)
707-829-0515 (international or local)
707-829-0104 (fax)

We have a web page for this book, where we list errata, examples, and any additional information. You can access this page at *http://bit.ly/gradle-recipes-for-android*.

To comment or ask technical questions about this book, send email to *bookquestions@oreilly.com*.

For more information about our books, courses, conferences, and news, see our website at *http://www.oreilly.com*.

Find us on Facebook: *http://facebook.com/oreilly*

Follow us on Twitter: *http://twitter.com/oreillymedia*

Watch us on YouTube: *http://www.youtube.com/oreillymedia*

Acknowledgments

The author would like to thank several members of Gradle, Inc. for their gracious help and assistance, including Hans Dockter, Luke Daley, Rooz Mohazabbi, and Cédric Champeau, among others. They are part of the reason both Gradle the technology and Gradle the company have such a bright future.

I also need to thank Xavier Ducrohet, head of the Android Studio team at Google as well as head of the Android plugin project. His hard work made both the IDE and the plugin a joy to use. I'm also glad he and his team haven't found time to update the online documentation sufficiently, leaving a great opening for this book.[1]

---

1 That was a joke. Honestly. But if you'd like to update the website now, I'm sure nobody will mind.

As a regular member of the No Fluff, Just Stuff conference series, I need to thank Jay Zimmerman for the opportunity to present on both Gradle- and Android-related topics many times over the years. I'm very happy to be part of No Fluff speaker community, many of whom have become good friends. I'm especially thinking of Nate Schutta, Raju Gandhi, Venkat Subramaniam, Neal Ford, Dan Hinojosa, Brian Sletten, Michael Carducci, and Craig Walls, but I could add another dozen names to that list without a problem. I'm also sure I'll hear about the people I didn't mention at my next No Fluff conference after they get around to reading this.

I'm also grateful to Matthew McCullough and Tim Berglund, the authors of the previous books of this series. Both men are friendly and helpful, and I'm honored to have my book included with theirs.

The reviewers for this book helped improve it considerably. I have to call out specifically the contributions of Andrew Reitz and James Harmon, who provided great insights into the technical parts of the book as well as its readability.

I have to mention my editors at O'Reilly, Meghan Blanchette and Brian Foster. Meghan was key in launching the book and helping edit the early stages, and Brian took over from her and shepherded it throughout the rest of the process. I'm grateful to the rest of the team at O'Reilly who helped throughout, even if I only vaguely understood the massive details that go into bringing a book to its final published form.

Even though it is ostensibly a competitor, the book *Gradle for Android* by Kevin Pelgrims (Packt Publishing) is excellent and taught me a lot. My book takes a different, recipe-based approach and is, of course, newer and therefore more up-to-date, but if you can do so I honestly recommend getting both.

Most of all I need to thank my wife Ginger and my son Xander for all the support they've given me over the years. I'm sorry again for getting involved in a book project so soon after finishing the previous one, and I promise I'll wait a while before starting the next one (probably).

Thank you, too, for reading the book. I hope you find it useful. Any errors or omissions are, of course, my own.

CHAPTER 1

Gradle for Android Basics

Android applications are built using the open source Gradle build system. Gradle is a state-of-the-art API that easily supports customizations and is widely used in the Java world. The Android plug-in for Gradle adds a wide range of features specific to Android apps, including build types, flavors, signing configurations, library projects, and more.

The recipes in this book cover the range of Gradle capabilities when applied to Android projects. Since the Android Studio IDE uses Gradle under the hood, special recipes are dedicated to it as well.

Hopefully the recipes in this book will help you configure and build whatever Android applications you desire.

1.1 Gradle Build Files in Android

Problem

You want to understand the generated Gradle build files for a new Android application.

Solution

Create a new Android project using Android Studio and review the files *settings.gradle, build.gradle*, and *app/build.gradle*.

Discussion

Android Studio is the only officially supported IDE for Android projects. To create a new Android project using Android Studio, use the "Start a new Android Studio project" wizard (Figure 1-1).

Figure 1-1. Android Studio Quick Start

The wizard prompts you for a project name and domain. You can use the Quick Start wizard to start a new Android Studio project named My Android App in the oreilly.com domain, as shown in Figure 1-2.

From here, select only the "Phone and Tablet" option and add a blank activity with the default name, MainActivity.

The name and type of activity does not affect the Gradle build files.

The resulting "Project" view in "Android" mode is shown in Figure 1-3, where the relevant Gradle files are highlighted.

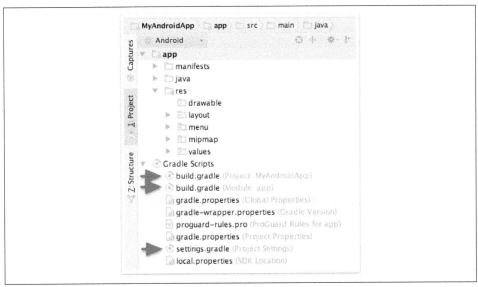

Figure 1-2. Create New Project wizard

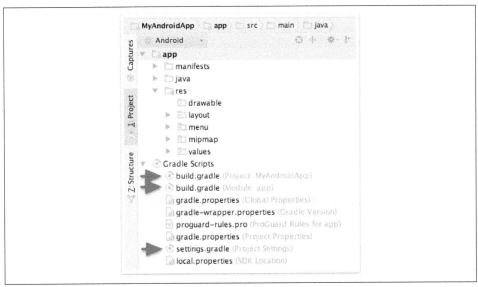

Figure 1-3. Project structure (Android view)

The project layout in the default (Project) view is shown in Figure 1-4.

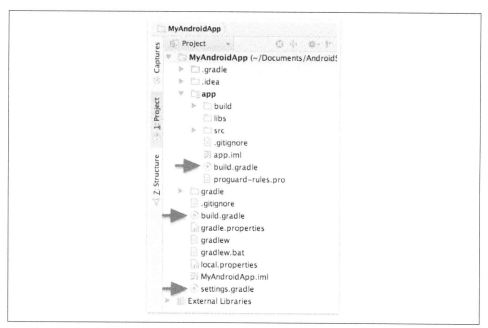

Figure 1-4. Project structure (Project view)

Android projects are multiproject Gradle builds. The *settings.gradle* file shows which subdirectories hold their own subprojects. The default file contents are shown in Example 1-1.

Example 1-1. settings.gradle

```
include ':app'
```

The `include` statement indicates that the *app* subdirectory is the only additional subproject. If you add an Android Library project, it too will be added to this file.

The top-level Gradle build file is in Example 1-2.

Example 1-2. Top-level build.gradle file

```
// Top-level build file where you can add configuration options
// common to all subprojects/modules.

buildscript {
    repositories {
        jcenter()
    }
    dependencies {
        classpath 'com.android.tools.build:gradle:2.0.0'
```

```
        // NOTE: Do not place your application dependencies here; they belong
        // in the individual module build.gradle files
    }
}

allprojects {
    repositories {
        jcenter()
    }
}

task clean(type: Delete) {
    delete rootProject.buildDir
}
```

The Gradle distribution does not include Android functionality by default. Google provides an Android plug-in for Gradle, which allows easy configuration of Android projects. The `buildscript` block in the top-level build file tells Gradle where to download that plug-in.

As you can see, by default the plug-in is downloaded from `jcenter`, which means the Bintray JCenter Artifactory repository. Other repositories are supported (especially `mavenCentral()`, the default Maven repository), but JCenter is now the default. All content from JCenter is served over a CDN with a secure HTTPS connection. It also tends to be faster.

The `allprojects` section indicates that the top-level project and any subprojects all default to using the `jcenter()` repository to resolve any Java library dependencies.

Gradle allows you to define tasks of your own and insert them into the directed acyclic graph (DAG), which Gradle uses to resolve task relationships. Here, a `clean` task has been added to the top-level build. The `type: Delete` part indicates that the new task is a customized instance of the built-in `Delete` task from Gradle. In this case, the task removes the build directory from the root project, which defaults to a *build* folder at the top level.

The Gradle build file for the `app` subproject is shown in Example 1-3.

Example 1-3. Gradle build file for the app subproject

```
apply plugin: 'com.android.application'

android {
    compileSdkVersion 23
    buildToolsVersion "23.0.3"

    defaultConfig {
        applicationId "com.kousenit.myandroidapp"
        minSdkVersion 19
```

```
        targetSdkVersion 23
        versionCode 1
        versionName "1.0"
    }
    buildTypes {
        release {
            minifyEnabled false
            proguardFiles getDefaultProguardFile('proguard-android.txt'),
                'proguard-rules.pro'
        }
    }
}

dependencies {
    compile fileTree(dir: 'libs', include: ['*.jar'])
    testCompile 'junit:junit:4.12'
    compile 'com.android.support:appcompat-v7:23.3.0'
}
```

The `apply` functionality in Gradle adds the Android plug-in to the build system, which enables the `android` section Domain Specific Language (DSL) configuration. This section is discussed in detail in Recipe 1.2.

The `dependencies` block consists of three lines. The first, `fileTree` dependency, means that all files ending in *.jar* in the *libs* folder are added to the compile classpath.

The second line tells Gradle to download version 4.12 of JUnit and add it to the "test compile" phase, meaning that JUnit classes will be available in the *src/androidTest/java* source tree, as well as the (optional) *src/test/java* tree, which can be added for pure unit tests (i.e., those that do not involve the Android API).

The third line tells Gradle to add version 23.3.0 of the `appcompat-v7 jar` files from the Android Support Libraries. Note that the `-v7` means support for Android applications back to version 7 of Android, not version 7 of the support library itself. The support library is listed as a `compile` dependency, so all of its classes are available throughout the project.

See Also

Links to all the relevant documentation sites are in Recipe 6.2. Dependencies are discussed in Recipe 1.5 and repositories are discussed in Recipe 1.7.

1.2 Configure SDK Versions and Other Defaults

Problem

You want to specify the minimum and target Android SDK versions and other default properties.

Solution

In the module Gradle build file, set values in the `android` block.

Discussion

The top-level Android build file adds the Android plug-in for Gradle to your project, via the `buildscript` block. Module build files "apply" the plug-in, which adds an `android` block to the Gradle DSL.

Inside the `android` block, you can specify several project properties, as shown in Example 1-4.

Example 1-4. Android block in build.gradle

```
apply plugin: 'com.android.application'

android {
    compileSdkVersion 23
    buildToolsVersion "23.0.3"

    defaultConfig {
        applicationId "com.kousenit.myandroidapp"
        minSdkVersion 19
        targetSdkVersion 23
        versionCode 1
        versionName "1.0"
    }
    compileOptions {
        sourceCompatibility JavaVersion.VERSION_1_7
        targetCompatibility JavaVersion.VERSION_1_7
    }
}
```

Regular Java projects use a `java` plug-in, but Android projects use the `com.android.application` plug-in instead.

> Do not apply the Java plug-in. This will cause build errors. Use the Android plug-in instead.

The `android` block is the entry point for the Android DSL. Here you must specify the compilation target using `compileSdkVersion` and the build tools version via `build ToolsVersion`. Both of these values should be assigned to the most recent available version, as they are backward compatible and include all current bug fixes.

The `defaultConfig` block inside `android` shows several properties:

applicationId

The "package" name of the application, which must be unique in the Google Play store. This value can never change during the life of your app; changing it will result in your app being treated as a brand new application, and existing users will not see changes as an update. Prior to the move to Gradle, this was the `pack age` attribute of the root element of the Android Manifest. The two can now be decoupled.

minSdkVersion

The minimum Android SDK version supported by this application. Devices earlier than this will not see this application when accessing the Google Play store.

targetSdkVersion

The version of Android intended for this application. Android Studio will issue a warning if this is anything other than the latest version, but you're free to use any version you like.

versionCode

An integer representing this version of your app relative to others. Apps normally use this during the upgrade process.

versionName

A string representing the release version of your app, shown to users. Normally in the form of a `<major>.<minor>.<version>` string, like most projects.

Prior to the switch to Gradle, the `minSdkVersion` and `buildToolsVersion` properties were specified in the Android Manifest as attributes of a `<uses-sdk>` tag. That approach is now deprecated, as the values there are overridden by the values in the Gradle build file.

The `compileOptions` section shows that this app expects to use JDK version 1.7.

In Android Studio, the Project Structure dialog shows the values in graphical form, shown in Figure 1-5.

The `defaultConfig` values are on the *Flavors* tab in the Project Structure window (Figure 1-6).

Documentation for the `defaultConfig` block, as with other elements of the DSL, can be found in the DSL reference (*http://bit.ly/gradle-dsl*).

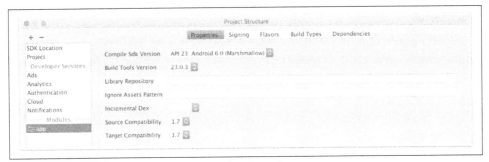

Figure 1-5. Project Structure view in Android Studio

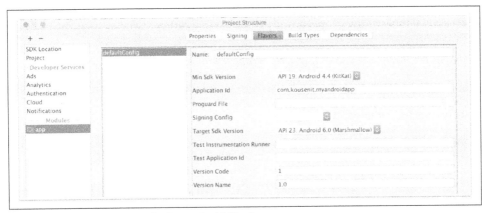

Figure 1-6. Properties inside the android block

See Also

Other child elements of `android`, like `buildTypes` or `productFlavors`, are discussed in Recipes Recipe 3.1, Recipe 3.2, Recipe 3.4, and more. The documentation links are given in Recipe 6.2.

1.3 Executing Gradle Builds from the Command Line

Problem

You want to run Gradle tasks from the command line.

Solution

From the command line, either use the provided Gradle wrapper or install Gradle and run it directly.

Discussion

You do not need to install Gradle in order to build Android projects. Android Studio comes with a Gradle distribution (in the form of a plug-in) and includes dedicated features to support it.

The term "Gradle wrapper" refers to the `gradlew` script for Unix and `gradlew.bat` script in the root directory of an Android application, where the ending "w" stands for "wrapper."

The purpose of the Gradle wrapper is to allow a client to run Gradle without having to install it first. The wrapper uses the *gradle-wrapper.jar* and the *gradle-wrapper.properties* files in the *gradle/wrapper* folder in the application root to start the process. A sample of the properties file is shown in Example 1-5.

Example 1-5. Keys and values in gradle-wrapper.properties

```
#Mon Dec 28 10:00:20 PST 2015
distributionBase=GRADLE_USER_HOME
distributionPath=wrapper/dists
zipStoreBase=GRADLE_USER_HOME
zipStorePath=wrapper/dists
distributionUrl=https\://services.gradle.org/distributions/gradle-2.10-all.zip
```

The `distributionUrl` property indicates that the wrapper will download and install version 2.10 of Gradle.[1] After the first run, the Gradle distribution will be cached in the `zipStorePath` folder under the `zipStoreBase` directory and then be available for all subsequent executions of Gradle tasks.

The wrapper is used at the command line simply by executing the `./gradlew` command on Unix or the `gradlew.bat` command on Windows (Example 1-6).

Example 1-6. Output from running the build task

```
> ./gradlew build
Downloading
https://services.gradle.org/distributions/gradle-2.10-all.zip
...............................................
....          (download of Gradle 2.10)      ....
...............................................
Unzipping /Users/kousen/.gradle/wrapper/dists/3i2gob.../gradle-2.10-all.zip
to /Users/kousen/.gradle/wrapper/dists/gradle-2.10-all/3i2gob...
Set executable permissions for:
/Users/kousen/.gradle/wrapper/dists/gradle-2.10-all/3i2gob.../gradle-2.10/bin/gradle
```

---

1 At the time of this writing, the current version of Gradle is 2.12. You can change the `distributionUrl` to include any legal Gradle version number.

```
Starting a new Gradle Daemon for this build (subsequent builds will be faster).
:app:preBuild UP-TO-DATE
:app:preDebugBuild UP-TO-DATE
... lots of tasks ...
:app:compileLint
:app:lint
Wrote HTML report to file:.../MyAndroidApp/app/build/outputs/lint-results.html
Wrote XML report to .../MyAndroidApp/app/build/outputs/lint-results.xml
:app:preDebugUnitTestBuild UP-TO-DATE
:app:prepareDebugUnitTestDependencies
... lots of tasks ...
:app:test
:app:check
:app:build

BUILD SUCCESSFUL

Total time: 51.352 secs // most of which was the download
```

 In this book, examples show the ./gradlew command for Unix-based operating systems. For Windows, simply replace that with gradlew or gradlew.bat without the dot-slash.

The initial download can take a few minutes, depending on your Internet connection speed. It only needs to be done once, however. After that, subsequent builds will use the cached version.

You can run any supported Gradle task, including your own custom tasks, at the command line. Compiled code will be found in the *app/build* folder. Generated *apk* (Android package) files are found in the *app/build/outputs/apk* directory.

The tasks command from Gradle shows what tasks are available in the build, as shown in Example 1-7.

Example 1-7. Output from tasks

```
:tasks

------------------------------------------------------------
All tasks runnable from root project
------------------------------------------------------------

Android tasks
------------
androidDependencies - Displays the Android dependencies of the project.
signingReport - Displays the signing info for each variant.
sourceSets - Prints out all the source sets defined in this project.
```

Build tasks
----
assemble - Assembles all variants of all applications and secondary packages.
assembleAndroidTest - Assembles all the Test applications.
assembleDebug - Assembles all Debug builds.
assembleRelease - Assembles all Release builds.
build - Assembles and tests this project.
buildDependents - Assembles and tests this project and all projects that depend on it.
buildNeeded - Assembles and tests this project and all projects it depends on.
compileDebugAndroidTestSources
compileDebugSources
compileDebugUnitTestSources
compileReleaseSources
compileReleaseUnitTestSources
mockableAndroidJar - Creates a version of android.jar that's suitable for unit tests.

Build Setup tasks
----
init - Initializes a new Gradle build. [incubating]
wrapper - Generates Gradle wrapper files. [incubating]

Help tasks
----
components - Displays the components produced by root project 'MyAndroidApp'.
dependencies - Displays all dependencies declared in root project 'MyAndroidApp'.
dependencyInsight - Displays the insight into a specific dependency in root
    project 'MyAndroidApp'.
help - Displays a help message.
model - Displays the configuration model of root project 'MyAndroidApp'. [incubating]
projects - Displays the subprojects of root project 'MyAndroidApp'.
properties - Displays the properties of root project 'MyAndroidApp'.
tasks - Displays the tasks runnable from root project 'MyAndroidApp'
    (some of the displayed tasks may belong to subprojects).

Install tasks
----
installDebug - Installs the Debug build.
installDebugAndroidTest - Installs the android (on device) tests for the Debug build.
uninstallAll - Uninstall all applications.
uninstallDebug - Uninstalls the Debug build.
uninstallDebugAndroidTest - Uninstalls the android (on device) tests for the build.
uninstallRelease - Uninstalls the Release build.

Verification tasks
----
check - Runs all checks.
clean - Deletes the build directory.
connectedAndroidTest - Installs and runs instrumentation tests for all flavors
    on connected devices.
connectedCheck - Runs all device checks on currently connected devices.
connectedDebugAndroidTest - Installs and runs the tests for debug connected devices.
deviceAndroidTest - Installs and runs instrumentation tests using all Providers.

```
deviceCheck - Runs all device checks using Device Providers and Test Servers.
lint - Runs lint on all variants.
lintDebug - Runs lint on the Debug build.
lintRelease - Runs lint on the Release build.
test - Run unit tests for all variants.
testDebugUnitTest - Run unit tests for the debug build.
testReleaseUnitTest - Run unit tests for the release build.

Other tasks
-----------
clean
jarDebugClasses
jarReleaseClasses
lintVitalRelease - Runs lint on just the fatal issues in the Release build.

To see all tasks and more detail, run gradlew tasks --all

To see more detail about a task, run gradlew help --task <task>

BUILD SUCCESSFUL
```

While this may seem like a lot of tasks, you actually use a small number in practice. When you add multiple build types and flavors to your project, the number will go up considerably.

Additional features and command-line flags

You can run multiple tasks by separating them by spaces, as in Example 1-8.

Example 1-8. Executing more than one task

```
> ./gradlew lint assembleDebug
```

Note that repeating the same task name only executes it once.

You can exclude a task by using the -x flag, as shown in Example 1-9.

Example 1-9. Excluding the lintDebug task

```
> ./gradlew assembleDebug -x lintDebug
```

The --all flag on the tasks command shows all the tasks in the project as well as the dependencies for each task.

> The output from gradle tasks --all can be very long.

You can abbreviate task names from the command line by providing just enough letters to uniquely determine it (Example 1-10).

Example 1-10. The dependency tree for each configuration

```
> ./gradlew anDep
:app:androidDependencies
debug
\--- com.android.support:appcompat-v7:23.3.0
     +--- com.android.support:support-vector-drawable:23.3.0
     |    \--- com.android.support:support-v4:23.3.0
     |         \--- LOCAL: internal_impl-23.3.0.jar
     +--- com.android.support:animated-vector-drawable:23.3.0
     |    \--- com.android.support:support-vector-drawable:23.3.0
     |         \--- com.android.support:support-v4:23.3.0
     |              \--- LOCAL: internal_impl-23.3.0.jar
     \--- com.android.support:support-v4:23.3.0
          \--- LOCAL: internal_impl-23.3.0.jar

debugAndroidTest
No dependencies

debugUnitTest
No dependencies

release
\--- com.android.support:appcompat-v7:23.3.0
     +--- com.android.support:support-vector-drawable:23.3.0
     |    \--- com.android.support:support-v4:23.3.0
     |         \--- LOCAL: internal_impl-23.3.0.jar
     +--- com.android.support:animated-vector-drawable:23.3.0
     |    \--- com.android.support:support-vector-drawable:23.3.0
     |         \--- com.android.support:support-v4:23.3.0
     |              \--- LOCAL: internal_impl-23.3.0.jar
     \--- com.android.support:support-v4:23.3.0
          \--- LOCAL: internal_impl-23.3.0.jar

releaseUnitTest
No dependencies

BUILD SUCCESSFUL
```

The camel-case notation (`anDep` for `androidDependencies`) works well, as long as the
resolution is unique (Example 1-11).

Example 1-11. Not enough letters to be unique

```
> ./gradlew pro

FAILURE: Build failed with an exception.

* What went wrong:
Task 'pro' is ambiguous in root project 'MyAndroidApp'. Candidates are:
'projects', 'properties'.
```

The error message shows exactly what went wrong: pro is ambiguous, since it matches both projects and properties. Just add another letter to make it unique.

Finally, if your build file is not called *build.gradle*, use the -b flag to specify the build filename (Example 1-12).

Example 1-12. Using a nondefault build filename

```
> ./gradlew -b app.gradle
```

See Also

Appendix B gives a summary of Gradle installation and features beyond Android projects. Recipe 1.5 discusses dependencies in the build file. Recipe 4.3 illustrates excluding tasks from the build process.

1.4 Executing Gradle Builds from Android Studio

Problem

You want to run Gradle from inside Android Studio.

Solution

Use the Gradle view to execute tasks.

Discussion

When you create an Android project, Android Studio generates Gradle build files for a multiproject build (discussed in Recipe 1.1). The IDE also provides a Gradle view that organizes all of its tasks, as shown in Figure 1-7.

Figure 1-7. Gradle view inside Android Studio

Gradle tasks are organized into categories, like android, build, install, and other, as Figure 1-7 illustrates.

To execute a particular task, double-click the entry in the Gradle window. The result is shown in Figure 1-8.

Double-clicking any task executes that task on the command line, which is shown in the Run window. Every time you run a particular task, a run configuration is created and stored under the Run Configurations menu, so running it again simply requires another double-click.

Figure 1-8. Running Gradle inside Android Studio

The execution seen in the Run window shows once again that the IDE is essentially just a frontend on Gradle. Any execution, from build to test to deployment, is actually executing Gradle tasks at the command line.

Android Studio also provides a Gradle Console view, as shown in Figure 1-9.

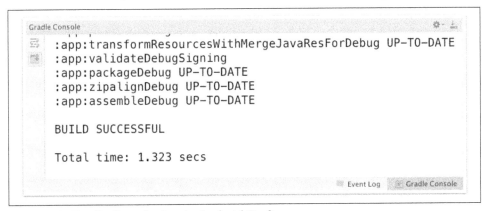

Figure 1-9. Gradle Console view in Android Studio

See Also

To run Gradle tasks from the command line using the included wrapper, refer to Recipe 1.3.

1.5 Adding Java Library Dependencies

Problem

You want to add additional Java libraries to your Android app.

Solution

Add the group, name, and version to the `dependencies` block in the *build.gradle* file included in your application module.

Discussion

By default, Android applications come with two *build.gradle* files: one at the top-level, and one for the application itself. The latter is normally stored in a subdirectory called *app*.

Inside the *build.gradle* file in the *app* directory, there is a block called `dependencies`. Example 1-13 shows a sample from a new Android application generated by Android Studio.

Example 1-13. Default dependencies in a new Android project

```
dependencies {
    compile fileTree(include: ['*.jar'], dir: 'libs')
    testCompile 'junit:junit:4.12'
    compile 'com.android.support:appcompat-v7:23.3.0'
}
```

Basic syntax

Gradle supports several different ways of listing dependencies. The most common is to use quotes with colon-separated group, name, and version values.

 Gradle files use Groovy, which supports both single- and double-quoted strings. Double quotes allow *interpolation*, or variable substitution, but are otherwise identical. See Appendix A for details.

Each dependency is associated with a *configuration*. Android projects include `compile`, `runtime`, `testCompile`, and `testRuntime` configurations. Plugins can add additional configurations, and you can also define your own.

The full syntax for a dependency calls out the group, name, and version numbers explicitly (Example 1-14).

Example 1-14. Full syntax for dependencies

```
testCompile group: 'junit', name: 'junit', version: '4.12'
```

The result of Example 1-14 is entirely equivalent to that in Example 1-15.

Example 1-15. Shortcut syntax for dependencies

```
testCompile 'junit:junit:4.12'
```

This is the shortcut form used in the default build file.

It is legal, though not recommended, to specify a version number with a plus sign, as shown in Example 1-16.

Example 1-16. Version number as a variable (not recommended)

```
testCompile 'junit:junit:4.+'
```

This tells Gradle that any version of JUnit greater than or equal to 4.0 is required to compile the project's tests. While this works, it makes the build less deterministic and therefore less reproducible. Explicit version numbers also protect you from changes in later versions of a particular API.

Favor explicit version numbers for dependencies. This protects you from later changes in dependent libraries and makes your build reproducible.

If you want to add a set of files to a configuration without adding them to a repository, you can use the `files` or `fileTree` syntax inside the `dependencies` block (Example 1-17).

Example 1-17. File and directory dependencies

```
dependencies {
    compile files('libs/a.jar', 'libs/b.jar')
    compile fileTree(dir: 'libs', include: '*.jar')
}
```

The last line uses the same syntax as that employed in the default Gradle build file.

Next, Gradle needs to know where to search to resolve dependencies. This is done through a `repositories` block.

Synchronizing the project

Android Studio monitors the Gradle build files and offers to synchronize new changes automatically.

For example, consider adding the Retrofit 2 project to *build.gradle* in the app project.

As Figure 1-10 shows, after any change to the *build.gradle* file, Android Studio offers to synchronize the project. This downloads any required libraries and adds them to the project.

Figure 1-10. Android Studio offering to synchronize project dependencies

After clicking the SycNow link, the downloaded libraries appear in the External Libraries section of the project window (Figure 1-11).

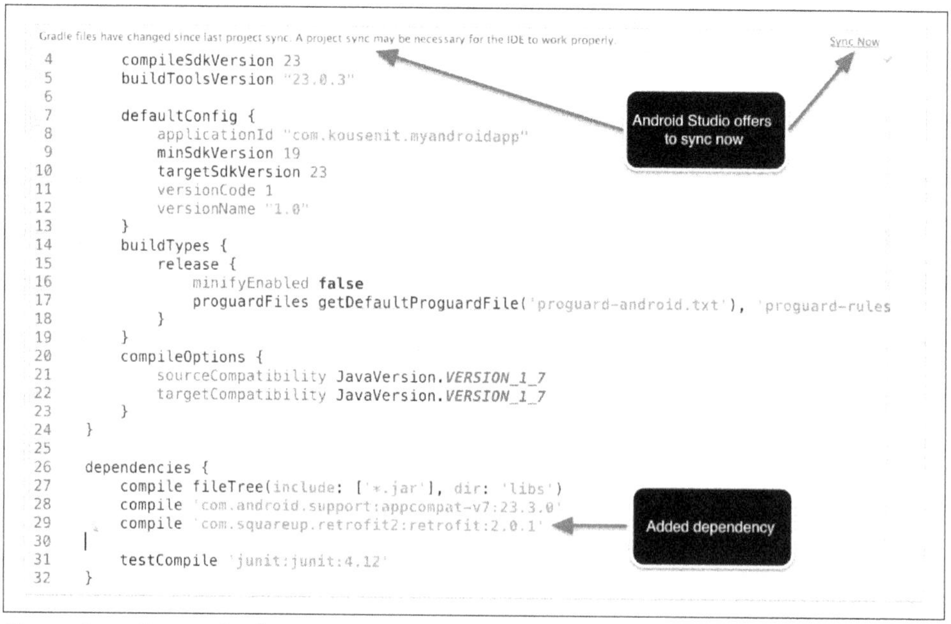

Figure 1-11. External Libraries

In this case, the retrofit dependency also added the okhttp and okio libraries as transitive dependencies, as shown in Figure 1-12.

If you miss your opportunity to click the Sync Now link, Android Studio provides a special icon in the toolbar for the same purpose, as well as a menu item.

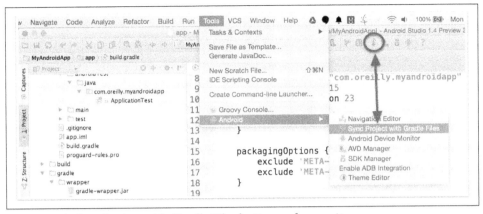

Figure 1-12. Sync Project with Gradle Files button and menu item

Transitive dependencies

There's an old joke that defines Maven as a DSL for downloading the Internet. If that is true for Maven, it's also true for Gradle. Both download transitive dependencies, which are libraries that themselves depend on other libraries.

In regular Java projects, the Gradle command `dependencies` can be used to see the transitive dependencies. Android projects use the `androidDependencies` command instead.

Consider the `dependencies` block from Example 1-13. Running the `androidDependen cies` task gives the output shown in Example 1-18.

Example 1-18. Seeing Android dependencies

```
> ./gradlew androidDependencies

:app:androidDependencies
debug
\--- com.android.support:appcompat-v7:23.3.0
    +--- com.android.support:support-vector-drawable:23.3.0
    |    \--- com.android.support:support-v4:23.3.0
    |         \--- LOCAL: internal_impl-23.3.0.jar
    +--- com.android.support:animated-vector-drawable:23.3.0
    |    \--- com.android.support:support-vector-drawable:23.3.0
    |         \--- com.android.support:support-v4:23.3.0
    |              \--- LOCAL: internal_impl-23.3.0.jar
    \--- com.android.support:support-v4:23.3.0
         \--- LOCAL: internal_impl-23.3.0.jar

debugAndroidTest
No dependencies
```

```
debugUnitTest
No dependencies

release
\--- com.android.support:appcompat-v7:23.3.0
     +--- com.android.support:support-vector-drawable:23.3.0
     |     \--- com.android.support:support-v4:23.3.0
     |           \--- LOCAL: internal_impl-23.3.0.jar
     +--- com.android.support:animated-vector-drawable:23.3.0
     |     \--- com.android.support:support-vector-drawable:23.3.0
     |           \--- com.android.support:support-v4:23.3.0
     |                 \--- LOCAL: internal_impl-23.3.0.jar
     \--- com.android.support:support-v4:23.3.0
           \--- LOCAL: internal_impl-23.3.0.jar

releaseUnitTest
No dependencies
```

The `debug` and `release` builds both use the `appcompat-v7` library from the Android Support libraries. That library depends on the `support-v4` library, among others, which uses an internal `jar` from the Android SDK.

Managing transitive dependencies manually sounds like a good idea until you actually try to do it. The complexity grows quickly and doesn't scale well. Gradle is very good at resolving versioning issues among dependencies.

Still, Gradle does provide a syntax for including and excluding individual libraries.

Gradle follows transitive dependencies by default. If you want to turn that off for a particular library, use the `transitive` flag (Example 1-19).

Example 1-19. Disabling transitive dependencies

```
dependencies {
    runtime group: 'com.squareup.retrofit2', name: 'retrofit', version: '2.0.1',
      transitive: false
}
```

Changing the value of the `transitive` flag to `false` prevents the download of transitive dependencies, so you'll have to add whatever is required yourself.

If you only want a module `jar`, without any additional dependencies, you can specify that as well (Example 1-20).

Example 1-20. Full syntax for module jar only

```
dependencies {
    compile 'org.codehaus.groovy:groovy-all:2.4.4@jar'  ❶
    compile group: 'org.codehaus.groovy', name: 'groovy-all',
```

```
      version: '2.4.4', ext: 'jar'  ❷
}
```

❶   Shortcut syntax

❷   Full version

The shortcut notation uses the @ sign, while the full version sets an ext (for exten-
sion) value.

You can also exclude a transitive dependency in the dependencies block
(Example 1-21).

Example 1-21. Excluding dependencies

```
dependencies {
  androidTestCompile('org.spockframework:spock-core:1.0-groovy-2.4') {
    exclude group: 'org.codehaus.groovy'
    exclude group: 'junit'
  }
}
```

In this case, the spock-core project excludes the Groovy dependency and the JUnit
library, both of which are includes by other means.

See Also

Recipe 1.6 shows how to add dependencies through the Android Studio IDE. Recipe
1.7 discusses repositories, which are used to resolve dependencies. Recipe 4.5 discusses the situation where one module depends on another, as with Android libraries.

1.6 Adding Library Dependencies Using Android Studio

Problem

Rather than edit the *build.config* file directly, you want to add dependencies using the
Android Studio IDE.

Solution

Use the *Project Structure* section of Android Studio, with the *Dependencies* tab.

Discussion

Experienced Gradle developers are comfortable editing the *build.gradle* file directly, but the IDE does not give you a lot of code assistance in doing so. The Project Structure display, however, gives a graphical view of the build file contents.

Access the Project Structure menu item under the File menu to see the overall display. Then select the module containing your application (`app` by default) as shown in Figure 1-13.

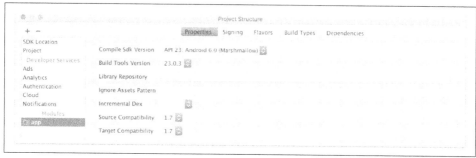

Figure 1-13. Project Structure UI (shown earlier in Figure 1-5)

Selecting `app` in the Modules section shows the default page, with the Properties tab highlighted. This shows, among other things, the Compile SDK Version and Build Tools Version.

Click the Dependencies tab to see any existing dependencies, along with the ability to add new ones (Figure 1-14).

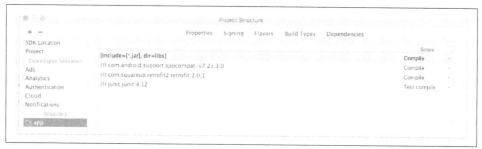

Figure 1-14. Dependencies tab in Project Structure

The "Scope" column allows you to specify the configuration where the dependency is needed. Current choices are:

- Compile
- Provided
- APK

- Test compile
- Debug compile
- Release compile

Clicking the plus button at the bottom of the window offers to add three different types of dependencies, as shown in Figure 1-15.

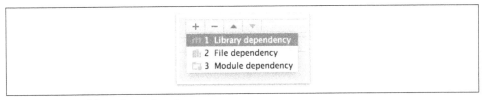

Figure 1-15. Adding dependencies pop-up

File dependencies allow you browse the filesystem for individual jar files. Module dependencies refer to other modules in the same project, which is discussed in the recipe for library projects.

The "Library Dependencies" option brings up a dialog box that allows you to search Maven Central for a particular dependency. By default it shows all the optional support libraries and Google Play services (Figure 1-16).

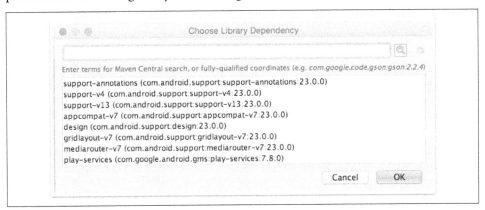

Figure 1-16. Choosing library dependencies

Enter a string in the search box and click the search icon (the magnifying glass in versions prior to 2.0 and the three dots in AS 2.0 and above) to find the full Maven coordinates of the dependency (Figure 1-17).

Clicking OK when you're done triggers a Gradle project sync, which downloads the dependency and adds it to your project.

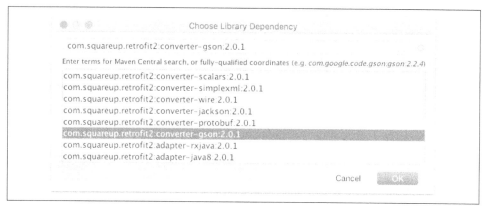

Figure 1-17. Finding the Gson library

See Also

Recipe 1.5 reviews how to add dependencies by editing the Gradle build files directly. Recipe 1.7 is about configuring Gradle repositories that are used to resolve the dependencies.

1.7 Configuring Repositories

Problem

You need Gradle to accurately resolve any library dependencies.

Solution

Configure the `repositories` block in your Gradle build file.

Discussion

Declaring Repositories

The `repositories` block tells Gradle where to find the dependencies. By default, Android uses either `jcenter()` or `mavenCentral()`, which represent the default Bintray JCenter repository and the public Maven Central Repository, respectively (Example 1-22).

Example 1-22. The default JCenter repository

```
repositories {
    jcenter()
}
```

This refers to the JCenter repository located at *https://jcenter.bintray.com*. Note that it uses HTTPS for the connection.

There are two shortcuts available for Maven repositories. The `mavenCentral()` syntax refers to the central Maven 2 repository at *http://repo1.maven.org/maven2*. The `maven Local()` syntax refers to your local Maven cache (Example 1-23).

Example 1-23. Built-in Maven repositories in the repositories block

```
repositories {
    mavenLocal()      ❶
    mavenCentral()    ❷
}
```

❶   Local Maven cache

❷   Public Maven Central respository

Any Maven repository can be added to the default list using a `maven` argument with a `url` block (Example 1-24).

Example 1-24. Adding a Maven repo from a URL

```
repositories {
    maven {
        url 'http://repo.spring.io/milestone'
    }
}
```

Password-protected repositories use a `credentials` block, as Example 1-25 (taken from the Gradle user guide) shows.

Example 1-25. Accessing a Maven repo requiring credentials

```
repositories {
    maven {
        credentials {
            username 'username'
            password 'password'
        }
        url 'http://repo.mycompany.com/maven2'
    }
}
```

You can move the explicit username and password values to a file called *gradle.prop-erties*. Recipe 2.1 discusses this in detail.

Ivy and local repositories are added using a similar syntax.

Example 1-26. Using an Ivy repository

```
repositories {
    ivy {
        url 'http://my.ivy.repo'
    }
}
```

If you have files on the local filesystem, you can use a directory as a repository with the flatDir syntax (Example 1-27).

Example 1-27. Using a local directory as a repository

```
repositories {
    flatDir {
        dirs 'lib'
    }
}
```

This is an alternative to adding the files explicitly to the dependencies block with files or fileTree.

You often will add multiple repositories to your build. Gradle will search each in turn, top down, until it resolves all of your dependencies.

See Also

Recipe 1.5 and Recipe 1.6 are about configuring the dependencies themselves.

CHAPTER 2

From Project Import to Release

2.1 Setting Project Properties

Problem

You want to add extra properties to your project, or externalize hardcoded values.

Solution

Use the `ext` block for common values. To remove them from the build file, put properties in the *gradle.properties* file, or set them on the command line using the `-P` flag.

Discussion

Gradle build files support property definitions using a simple `ext` syntax, where in this case "ext" stands for "extra." This makes it easy to define a variable value once and use it throughout the file.

These properties can be hardcoded into the build file if you wish. Example 2-1 is a sample from a Gradle build file from the Android Annotations project (*http://androi dannotations.org*).

Example 2-1. Sample "extra" property

```
ext {
    def AAVersion = '4.0-SNAPSHOT' // change this to your desired version
}

dependencies {
    apt "org.androidannotations:androidannotations:$AAVersion"
```

```
    compile "org.androidannotations:androidannotations-api:$AAVersion"
}
```

Normal Groovy idioms apply here, meaning that the variable AAVersion is untyped but takes on a String value at assignment, and that the variable is interpolated into the two Groovy string dependencies.

The use of the def keyword here implies that this is a local variable in the current build file. Defining the variable without def (or any other type) adds the variable as an attribute of the project object, making it available in this project as well as any of its subprojects.

 An untyped variable in the ext block adds properties to the Project instance associated with the build.

What if, however, you wished to remove the actual value from the build file? Consider a Maven repository with login credentials, as shown in Example 2-2.

Example 2-2. Maven repo with credentials

```
repositories {
    maven {
        url 'http://repo.mycompany.com/maven2'
        credentials {
            username 'user'      ❶
            password 'password'  ❶
        }
    }
}
```

❶ Hardcoded values

You probably don't want to keep the actual username and password values in the build file. Instead, add them to the *gradle.properties* file in the project root, as shown in Example 2-3.

Example 2-3. gradle.properties file

```
login='user'
pass='my_long_and_highly_complex_password'
```

Now the credentials block in Example 2-2 can be replaced with variables, as in Example 2-4.

Example 2-4. Revised Maven repo with explicit credentials removed

```
repositories {
    maven {
        url 'http://repo.mycompany.com/maven2'
        credentials {
            username login   ❶
            password pass     ❶
        }
    }
}
```

❶ Variables supplied from *gradle.properties* or on the command line

You also have the option of setting the value of properties on the command line, by using the -P argument to gradle (Example 2-5).

Example 2-5. Running gradle with the -P flag

```
> gradle -Plogin=me -Ppassword=this_is_my_password assembleDebug
```

To demonstrate what happens when you use multiple approaches, consider a build file as in Example 2-6.

Example 2-6. Making properties dynamic

```
ext {
    if (!project.hasProperty('user')) {   ❶
        user = 'user_from_build_file'
    }
    if (!project.hasProperty('pass')) {   ❶
        pass = 'pass_from_build_file'
    }
}

task printProperties() {   ❷
    doLast {
        println "username=$user"
        println "password=$pass"
    }
}
```

❶ Checking if project properties exist

❷ Custom task to print property values

Executing the `printProperties` task without any external configuration gives the values set in the ext block (Example 2-7).

Example 2-7. Output from running Gradle with ext values

```
> ./gradlew printProperties
:app:printProperties
username=user_from_build_file
password=pass_from_build_file
```

If the values are set in the *gradle.properties* file in the project root, the result is different (Examples 2-8 and 2-9).

Example 2-8. Using gradle.properties to set user and pass values

```
user=user_from_gradle_properties
pass=pass_from_gradle_properties
```

Example 2-9. Output from running Gradle with properties from gradle.properties

```
> ./gradlew printProperties
:app:printProperties
username=user_from_gradle_properties
password=pass_from_gradle_properties
```

The values can also be set from the command line, which takes top precedence (Example 2-10).

Example 2-10. Running Gradle with properties set from command line

```
> ./gradlew -Puser=user_from_pflag -Ppass=pass_from_pflag printProperties
:app:printProperties
username=user_from_pflag
password=pass_from_pflag
```

The combination of "extras" block, properties file, and command-line flag will hopefully give you enough options to accomplish whatever you need.

See Also

Custom tasks are discussed in Recipe 4.1. Setting up repositories is part of Recipe 1.7.

2.2 Porting Apps from Eclipse ADT to Android Studio

Problem

You want to import an existing Eclipse ADT project to Android Studio.

Solution

Android Studio provides an "import" wizard that rewrites existing projects.

Discussion

Figure 2-1 shows the link on the Android Studio welcome page for importing a project from either Eclipse ADT or Gradle.

Figure 2-1. Android Studio welcome page showing the import project option

The link brings up a view where you can navigate to an existing Eclipse ADT project. Figure 2-2 shows such a project. It uses the old project structure, where res, src, and AndroidManifest.xml are all direct children of the root.

After choosing a destination directory (the wizard does not overwrite the original project), the wizard offers to convert jar files in the *lib* folder into dependencies in the Gradle build file, among other options, as shown in Figure 2-3.

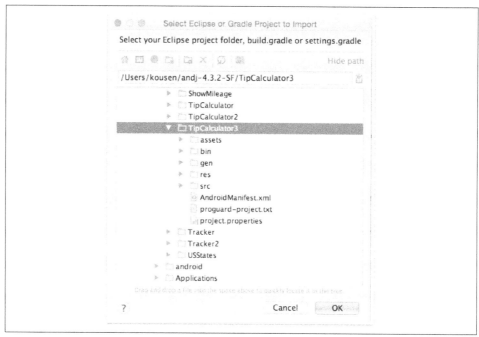

Figure 2-2. Select Eclipse ADT project

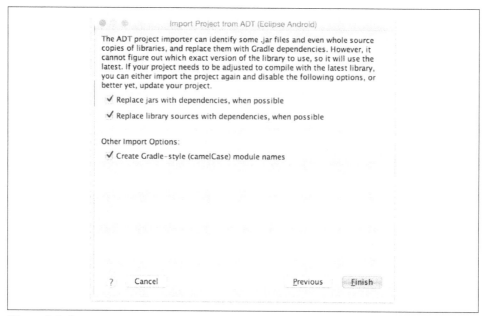

Figure 2-3. Import project options

The wizard then restructures the project and builds it. By default, an import-summary.txt window shows the major changes. Example 2-11 shows a sample.

Example 2-11. Project Import Summary text file

```
ECLIPSE ANDROID PROJECT IMPORT SUMMARY
======================================

Ignored Files:
--------------
The following files were *not* copied into the new Gradle project; you
should evaluate whether these are still needed in your project and if
so manually move them:

* proguard-project.txt

Moved Files:
------------
Android Gradle projects use a different directory structure than ADT
Eclipse projects. Here's how the projects were restructured:

* AndroidManifest.xml => app/src/main/AndroidManifest.xml
* assets/ => app/src/main/assets
* res/ => app/src/main/res/
* src/ => app/src/main/java/

Next Steps:
-----------
You can now build the project. The Gradle project needs network
connectivity to download dependencies.

Bugs:
-----
If for some reason your project does not build, and you determine that
it is due to a bug or limitation of the Eclipse to Gradle importer,
please file a bug at http://b.android.com with category
Component-Tools.

(This import summary is for your information only, and can be deleted
after import once you are satisfied with the results.)
```

Other than the ProGuard file recommendation, the rest of the changes are mostly moving files around.

The generated top-level *gradle.build* file is the same as when you create a new project, as in Example 2-12.

Example 2-12. Top-level generated build file

```
sub-projects/modules.
buildscript {
    repositories {
        jcenter()
    }
    dependencies {
        classpath 'com.android.tools.build:gradle:2.0.0'
    }
}

allprojects {
    repositories {
        jcenter()
    }
}
```

The *app* folder contains the original project, with a result similar to Example 2-13.

Example 2-13. App-level build file

```
apply plugin: 'com.android.application'

android {
    compileSdkVersion 17
    buildToolsVersion "23.0.3"

    defaultConfig {
        applicationId "com.example.tips"
        minSdkVersion 8
        targetSdkVersion 17
    }

    buildTypes {
        release {
            minifyEnabled false
            proguardFiles getDefaultProguardFile('proguard-android.txt'),
                'proguard-rules.txt'
        }
    }
}
```

(Note that this particular project didn't have any additional `jar` files, so no added `dependencies` block was required.)

Finally, a *settings.gradle* file was generated (Example 2-14), which shows that the `app` project is the only included module.

Example 2-14. Generated settings.gradle file

```
include ':app'
```

While the *AndroidManifest.xml* file has not been changed, opening it in Android Studio does give you a couple of warnings (Example 2-15).

Example 2-15. Warnings in AndroidManifest.xml

```
<?xml version="1.0" encoding="utf-8"?>
<manifest xmlns:android="http://schemas.android.com/apk/res/android"
    package="com.example.tips"
    android:versionCode="1"
    android:versionName="1.0" >

    <uses-sdk
        android:minSdkVersion="8"
        android:targetSdkVersion="17" />     ❶

    <application
      <!-- no problems --!>
    </application>
</manifest>
```

❶   Multiple warnings

Android Studio warns you that the `targetSdkVersion` is set to an older version of the Android SDK. It also points out that the values of `minSdkVersion` and `targetSdkVersion` are overridden by their counterparts in the Gradle build file (Example 1-3).

Since the Gradle build wins, the best approach is to simply delete the `uses-sdk` tag from the manifest, and then change the values in the *build.gradle* file if desired.

See Also

Recipe 4.4 discusses the `sourceSets` property in Gradle. Recipe 2.3 shows how the ADT plug-in in Eclipse can generate a Gradle build file mapping the older structure.

2.3 Porting Apps from Eclipse ADT Using Eclipse

Problem

You want to export an existing Eclipse ADT project using Gradle.

Solution

The Eclipse ADT plug-in can generate a Gradle build for you.

Discussion

The Android Developer Tools (ADT) plug-in for Eclipse was the primary IDE for building Android projects before the Gradle build process was introduced in 2013. The ADT project is now deprecated in favor of Android Studio, but legacy projects do, of course, exist.

The ADT plug-in can generate a Gradle build file for you based on the existing project structure and dependencies.

 The preferred way to port a project from ADT to Android Studio is to use the import wizard from Android Studio. The export process shown here is no longer recommended.

Since this is no longer the preferred porting mechanism, it is being shown here because you may encounter such projects in practice. It's also a good example of a Gradle sourceSet mapping, which shows how to map the old project structure to the new Gradle-based layout.

The Eclipse ADT structure put all source code in a directory called *src* under the project root. Resources were also in a *res* folder in the root. The Android manifest itself was also in the root directory. All of these locations changed in the new project structure.

The ADT plug-in can generate the Gradle build for you. Example 2-16 shows a section from one of those conversions.

Example 2-16. Mapping the old project structure to the new one

```
android {
    compileSdkVersion 18
    buildToolsVersion "17.0.0"

    defaultConfig {
        minSdkVersion 10
        targetSdkVersion 17
    }

    sourceSets {
        main {
            manifest.srcFile 'AndroidManifest.xml'
            java.srcDirs = ['src']
            resources.srcDirs = ['src']
            aild.ext.srcDirs = ['src']
            renderscript.srcDirs = ['src']
            res.srcDirs = ['res']
```

```
            assets.srcDirs = ['assets']
        }
    }
}
```

You can see based on the SDK versions that this was done some time ago, but the interesting part is the mapping done inside the `sourceSets` block. The new project structure expects *src/main/java* for source code. The existing project has an *src* folder in the root of the project. Therefore the `sourceSets` block maps *src/main/java* to *src* using the `srcDirs` property. In fact, all the folders have been mapped from the old project structure to the new one using this mechanism.

What you'll often see in these types of mappings is also a change for the tests folder and build types, as in Example 2-17.

Example 2-17. Changing the test and build type roots

```
sourceSets {
    main {
        manifest.srcFile 'AndroidManifest.xml'
        java.srcDirs = ['src']
        resources.srcDirs = ['src']
        aidl.srcDirs = ['src']
        renderscript.srcDirs = ['src']
        res.srcDirs = ['res']
        assets.srcDirs = ['assets']
    }

    // Move the tests to tests/java, tests/res, etc...
    instrumentTest.setRoot('tests')

    // Move the build types to build-types/<type>
    // For instance, build-types/debug/java, ...
    // This moves them out of them default location under src/<type>/...
    // which would conflict with src/ being used by the main source set.
    // Adding new build types or product flavors should be accompanied
    // by a similar customization.
    debug.setRoot('build-types/debug')
    release.setRoot('build-types/release')
}
```

The comments in the build file were actually added by the Eclipse ADT tool as part of the conversion process.

See Also

Recipe 4.4 discusses the `sourceSets` property in more detail.

2.4 Upgrading to a Newer Version of Gradle

Problem

You need to change the version of Gradle used by your application.

Solution

Generate a new wrapper, or modify the properties file directly.

Discussion

Android Studio includes a Gradle distribution. When you create a new Android application, the IDE automatically generates a *gradlew* script for Unix and a *gradlew.bat* file for Windows. These are the "wrapper" scripts that allow you to use Gradle without manually installing it first. Instead, the wrapper scripts download and install a version of Gradle for you.

Software projects last a long time, however, and Gradle releases new versions on a regular basis. You may wish to update the Gradle version used in your project, either for performance reasons (each new version is faster) or because new features were added to the project. To do so, you have two primary options:

1. Add a `wrapper` task to your *build.gradle* file and generate new wrapper scripts
2. Edit the `distributionUrl` value in *gradle-wrapper.properties* directly

The first option works best if your project already loads with the current version of Gradle. By default, Gradle builds already include a so-called `wrapper` task, which you can see by running the `gradle tasks` command, as in Example 2-18.

Example 2-18. The wrapper task in the list of tasks

```
> ./gradlew tasks

------------------------------------------------------------
All tasks runnable from root project
------------------------------------------------------------

// ...

Build Setup tasks
-----------------
wrapper - Generates Gradle wrapper files. [incubating] ❶

// ...
```

```
BUILD SUCCESSFUL
```

❶ Built-in `wrapper` task

The `gradle wrapper` command supports a `--gradle-version` argument. Therefore, one way to regenerate the wrapper with the desired version is shown in Example 2-19.

Example 2-19. Specifing the wrapper version on the command line

```
> ./gradlew wrapper --gradle-version 2.12
:wrapper

BUILD SUCCESSFUL
Total time: ... sec
```

The other option is to explicitly add the `wrapper` task to the (top-level) build file, and specify a value for `gradleVersion`, as shown in Example 2-20.

Example 2-20. Explicit Gradle wrapper task in top-level build.gradle file

```
task wrapper(type: Wrapper) {
    gradleVersion = 2.12
}
```

With this change, running the `./gradlew wrapper` task will generate the new wrapper files.

Every once in a while, however, the existing wrapper is so old that Android Studio refuses to sync with the existing the build files, making it impossible to run any tasks. In that case, you can always go directly to the files that control the wrapper, which are generated by the wrapper when it first runs.

In addition to the generated scripts *gradlew* and *gradlew.bat*, the wrapper relies on a folder called *gradle/wrapper* and the two files included there, *gradle-wrapper.jar* and *gradle-wrapper.properties*, as shown in Example 2-21.

Example 2-21. The Gradle wrapper files

```
gradlew
gradlew.bat
gradle/wrapper/
    gradle-wrapper.jar
    gradle-wrapper.properties
```

The *gradle-wrapper.properties* file, shown in Example 2-22, contains the `distribu`
`tionUrl` property, which tells the wrapper where to download the needed Gradle version.

Example 2-22. Properties in the gradle-wrapper.properties file

```
#... date of most recent update ...
distributionBase=GRADLE_USER_HOME
distributionPath=wrapper/dists
zipStoreBase=GRADLE_USER_HOME
zipStorePath=wrapper/dists
distributionUrl=https\://services.gradle.org/distributions/gradle-2.12-bin.zip
```

Feed free to edit this file directly, changing the version number in the `distribution`
`Url` property to whatever you prefer. That should allow you to run the existing wrapper scripts without a problem.

Upgrading Gradle with either the command-line flag or from the explicit `wrapper`
task adds only the binary distribution (note the `bin` value in the URL). Android Studio will then offer to download the complete distribution, including sources, with a
prompt shown in Figure 2-4.

Figure 2-4. Android Studio offering to upgrade to the source distribution

When you click the link, the value in the `distributionUrl` property in *gradle-*
wrapper.properties changes to the *all* version, as shown in Example 2-23.

Example 2-23. Upgraded properties in the gradle-wrapper.properties file

```
#... date of most recent update ...
distributionBase=GRADLE_USER_HOME
distributionPath=wrapper/dists
zipStoreBase=GRADLE_USER_HOME
zipStorePath=wrapper/dists
distributionUrl=https\://services.gradle.org/distributions/gradle-2.12-all.zip ❶
```

❶ Distribution now uses the `all` version, which includes sources

If you miss the opportunity to click the upgrade link, you can always modify the file
directly, replacing `bin` with `all` in the URL.

2.5 Sharing Settings Among Projects

Problem

You want to remove duplicated settings from multiple modules.

Solution

Use `allprojects` or `subprojects` blocks in your top-level Gradle build file.

Discussion

When you create a new Android project in Android Studio, the IDE creates a Gradle multiproject build with two build files: one at the top level, and one in a module called app. The top-level *build.gradle* file often has a block called `allprojects`, as in Example 2-24.

Example 2-24. The allprojects block in the top-level Gradle build file

```
allprojects {
    repositories {
        jcenter()
    }
}
```

This block comes from the Gradle DSL and thus works for all Gradle-based projects, not just Android projects. The `allprojects` property comes from the Project API in Gradle, where it is a property of the `org.gradle.api.Project` class. The property consists of a set containing the current project and all of its subprojects. There is also a method of the same name, which allows you configure the current project and all of its subprojects.

 It is common in the Gradle API to have a property and a method with the same name. The context determines which you are using.

The behavior is to apply the closure argument to each project returned by the `allpro jects` collection, which for a default project means the top-level project and the app module. In this case, it simply means that you don't need to repeat the `repositories` block in the app module, because it's already set.

An alternative is to use a subprojects block. For example, if you have multiple Android library projects, each will need to apply the library plug-in in their own build files. If all of your subprojects are Android libraries, you can remove the duplication by applying the plug-in at the top level, as in Example 2-25.

Example 2-25. Using a subprojects block in the top-level build file

```
subprojects {
    apply plugin: 'com.android.library'
}
```

As you might expect, the subprojects property returns the set of subprojects, and the subprojects method applies the supplied closure to each of them.

Advanced considerations

If you check the documentation for the allprojects method in Project (see Recipe 6.2 for documentation links) using the Gradle DSL reference, you'll find that the method takes a reference of type org.gradle.api.Action as an argument.

More specifically, the signature for the allprojects method is given in Example 2-26.

Example 2-26. The complete signature of the allprojects method in Project

```
void allprojects(Action<? super Project> action)
```

The documentation says that this method executes the given Action against this project and each of its subprojects. Action<T> is an interface with a single method, called execute, that takes a single generic argument, so the docs seem to imply that you have to create a class that implements the Action interface, instantiate it, and supply the result as an argument. In Java (prior to Java SE 8), this is often done as an anonymous inner class (Example 2-27).

Example 2-27. Implementing allprojects in Java, using an anonymous inner class

```
project.allprojects(new Action<Project>() {
    void execute(Project p) {
        // do whatever you like with the project
    }
});
```

In Groovy, you can implement a single-method interface simply by supplying a closure as an argument. The closure will then become the implementation of the method. The Gradle implementation of the allprojects and subprojects methods is to invoke the closure argument on each project in the collection.

If you look at the block in Example 2-24, you can see the result: the code is providing a closure to the `allprojects` method that says to configure the `repositories` block to use `jcenter()` as its repository.

Note that Java SE 8 introduced lambdas that work in a similar fashion. Java 8 lambdas can be assigned to so-called *functional interfaces*, which are interfaces containing only a single, abstract method. Groovy has had closures from the beginning of the language.

 Gradle 2.0 and above support Java SE 8. The Android SDK, however, still does not, though some lambda capabilities are planned for Android N as well as Android Studio version 2.1 that support it.

See Also

More details can be found in the Gradle source code (*http://github.com/gradle/gradle*).

2.6 Signing a Release APK

Problem

You need to digitally sign an APK so it can be released to the Google Play store.

Solution

Use Java's `keytool` command to create a certificate and configure its use in the `signingConfigs` block of your Gradle build file.

Discussion

All Android package (APK) files need to be digitally signed before they are deployed. By default, Android signs debug APKs for you, using a known key. To see this, you can use the `keytool` command from Java.

By default, the debug keystore resides in a subdirectory called *.android* in your home directory. The default name for the keystore is `debug.keystore`, and has a keystore password of `android`. Example 2-28 shows how to list the default certificate.

Example 2-28. Listing the key in the debug keystore (Mac OS X)

```
> cd ~/.android
> keytool -list -keystore debug.keystore
Enter keystore password:  ("android")

Keystore type: JKS
Keystore provider: SUN

Your keystore contains 1 entry

androiddebugkey, Feb 9, 2013, PrivateKeyEntry,
Certificate fingerprint (SHA1):
B7:39:B5:80:BE:A0:0D:6C:84:4F:A1:1F:4B:A1:00:14:12:25:DA:14
```

The keystore type is JKS, which stands for (naturally enough) Java KeyStore, used for public and private keys. Java supports another type called JCEKS (Java Cryptography Extensions KeyStore), which can be used for shared keys, but isn't used for Android applications.

The keystore has a self-signed certificate with an alias of androiddebugkey, which is used to sign debug APKs when they are deployed to connected devices or emulators.

 To reset the debug keystore, simply delete the file *debug.keystore*. It will be re-created next time you deploy an app.

You cannot deploy a release version of an app until you can sign it, which means generating a release key. This also uses the keytool utility. A sample run is shown in Example 2-29.

Example 2-29. Generating a release key

```
keytool -genkey -v -keystore myapp.keystore -alias my_alias
    -keyalg RSA -keysize 2048 -validity 10000  (all on one line)
Enter keystore password:  (probably shouldn't use use "password")
Re-enter new password:    (but if you did, type it again)
What is your first and last name?
  [Unknown]:  Ken Kousen
What is the name of your organizational unit?
  [Unknown]:
What is the name of your organization?
  [Unknown]:  Kousen IT, Inc.
What is the name of your City or Locality?
  [Unknown]:  Marlborough
What is the name of your State or Province?
```

```
   [Unknown]:  CT
What is the two-letter country code for this unit?
   [Unknown]:  US
Is CN=Ken Kousen, OU=Unknown, O="Kousen IT, Inc.", L=Marlborough,
  ST=CT, C=US correct?
   [no]:  yes

Generating 2,048 bit RSA key pair and self-signed certificate (SHA256withRSA)
  with a validity of 10,000 days for: CN=Ken Kousen, OU=Unknown,
  O="Kousen IT, Inc.", L=Marlborough, ST=CT, C=US
Enter key password for <my_alias>
        (RETURN if same as keystore password):
[Storing myapp.keystore]
```

The RSA algorithm is used to generate the public/private keypair, of 2K size, signed with the SHA256 algorithm, valid for 10,000 days (a bit over 27 years).

You could now use the `jarsigner` and `zipalign` tools to sign your APK, but it's easier to let Gradle do it.

As a child of the `android` closure, add a `signingConfigs` block, as shown in Example 2-30.

Example 2-30. A signingConfigs block in the module build file

```
android {
    // ... other sections ...

    signingConfigs {
        release {
            keyAlias 'my_alias'
            keyPassword 'password'
            storeFile file('/Users/kousen/keystores/myapp.keystore')
            storePassword 'password'
        }
    }
}
```

You probably don't want to put the passwords as hardcoded constants in the build file. Fortunately, you can put them in the *gradle.properties* file or set them on the command line. For details, see Recipe 2.1.

From the DSL documentation, the `signingConfigs` block delegates to an instance of the `SigningConfig` class, which has the four commonly used properties listed:

keyAlias
    The value used in the `keytool` when signing a particular key

keyPassword
    A particular key's password used during the signing process

storeFile

The disk file containing keys and certificates, generated by the `keytool`

storePassword

The password used for the keystore itself

There is also a `storeType` property (defaults to JKS, as shown in Example 2-29), but that is rarely used.

To make use of the new configuration, add a `signingConfig` property to the `release` build type (Example 2-31).

Example 2-31. Using a signing config in a release build

```
android {
    // ... other sections ...

    buildTypes {
        release {
            // ... other settings ...
            signingConfig signingConfigs.release
        }
    }
}
```

When you invoke the `assembleRelease` task from Gradle, the build will generate a release APK in the *app/build/outputs/apk* folder (Example 2-32).

Example 2-32. Running the assembleRelease task

```
> ./gradlew assembleRelease
:app:preBuild UP-TO-DATE
:app:preReleaseBuild UP-TO-DATE
// ... lots of tasks ...
:app:zipalignRelease UP-TO-DATE
:app:assembleRelease UP-TO-DATE

BUILD SUCCESSFUL

kousen at krakatoa in ~/Documents/AndroIDstudio/MyAndroidApp
> ls -l app/build/outputs/apk
total 12088
-rw-r--r--  1 kousen  staff  1275604 Aug 24 15:05 app-debug.apk
-rw-r--r--  1 kousen  staff  1275481 Aug 26 21:04 app-release.apk
```

Note—and this is important—*do not lose the keystore*. If you do, you will not be able to publish any updates to your app, since all versions must be signed with the same key.

All versions of an app must be signed with the same key. Otherwise new versions will be treated as completely new apps.

Put your keystore in a safe place. Yes, you're using self-signed certificates, but this is not done for encryption purposes. It's being used for integrity (guaranteeing that an APK has not been modified) and nonrepudiation (guaranteeing that you are the only one who could have signed it). If someone else gains access to your keystore, they could sign other apps in your name.

See Also

Recipe 2.7 discusses the same process using Android Studio dialogs.

2.7 Signing a Release APK Using Android Studio

Problem

You want to use Android Studio to generate signing configurations and assign them to build types.

Solution

The Build menu has options for generating signing configs, and the Project Structure dialog has tabs for assigning them to build types and flavors.

Discussion

Android Studio allows you to generate a keystore using the Build → Generate Signed APK menu option (Figure 2-5).

Figure 2-5. Generate Signed APK pop-up

Clicking "Create new…" brings up a pop-up to specify the location of the keystore and to generate a key pair (Figure 2-6).

Figure 2-6. New Key Store pop-up

If you choose an existing keystore, you can complete the passwords and alias to use an existing key inside it or create a new one, as in Figure 2-7.

Figure 2-7. Using an existing keystore

Once a self-signed certificate has been generated, the Project Structure dialog can be used to configure it for the current build. First, complete the values in the Signing tab, as in Figure 2-8.

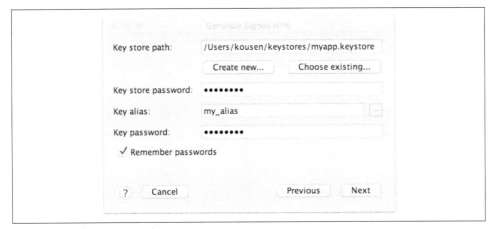

Figure 2-8. The Signing tab

Then associate a signing config with a particular build type using the Build Types tab (Figure 2-9).

Figure 2-9. Associating a signing config with a build type

A similar dialog can be used to sign particular flavors, which is dicussed in the recipe on flavors.

See Also

Recipe 2.6 shows how to generate keys from the command line and how to edit the relevant sections of the module build file directly.

CHAPTER 3

Build Types and Flavors

3.1 Working with Build Types

Problem

You want to customize the debug and release build types, or create additional types of your own.

Solution

The `buildTypes` block inside `android` is used to configure build types.

Discussion

A build type determines how an app is packaged. By default, the Android plug-in for Gradle supports two different types of builds: `debug` and `release`. Both can be configured inside the `buildTypes` block inside of the module build file. The `buildTypes` block from the module build file in a new project is shown in Example 3-1.

Example 3-1. Default buildTypes block from module build file

```
android {
    buildTypes {
        release {
            minifyEnabled false
            proguardFiles getDefaultProguardFile('proguard-android.txt'),
                'proguard-rules.pro'
        }
    }
}
```

The only build type shown in the example is the release build, but it is just as easy to add a debug block as well if you want to configure the default settings. Either block supports a range of properties. The complete set of properties and methods can be found in the DSL reference for the com.android.build.gradle.inter nal.dsl.BuildType class (*http://bit.ly/gradle-dsl*).

In the release block on the example, minifyEnabled refers to the automatic removal of unused resources in the packaged app. If true, Gradle also removes resources from dependent libraries if they are not needed. This only works if the shrinkResources property is also set to true.

In Example 3-2, both are set to true.

Example 3-2. Removing resources and shrinking code

```
android {
    buildTypes {
        release {
            minifyEnabled true      ❶
            shrinkResources true    ❷
            proguardFiles getDefaultProguardFile('proguard-android.txt'),
                'proguard-rules.pro'
        }
    }
}
```

❶ Turn on code shrinking

❷ Turn on resource shrinking

See the "Resource Shrinking" page (*http://bit.ly/resource-shrinking*) for further details.

Another property available in build types is debuggable. Debug builds automatically have debuggable set to true, while all other builds default to false.

In order to install multiple build types on a single device, Android must be able to distinguish their application IDs. The applicationIDsuffix property allows Gradle to generate multiple APKs, each with its own ID (Example 3-3).

Example 3-3. Adding a suffix to the application ID and version name

```
android {
    // ... other properties ...
    buildTypes {
        debug {
            applicationIDsuffix '.debug'
            versionNameSuffix '-debug'
        }
```

```
        // .. other build types ...
    }
}
```

Now both a release and a debug version of the app can be deployed to the same device. If you access the Settings on the device and go to Apps, you can see that both the debug and release versions are on the same app (Figure 3-1).

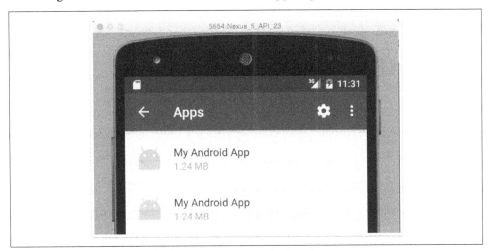

Figure 3-1. Both debug and release versions are deployed

To distinguish them, select each version and view the full version name in the "App info" settings, as in Figure 3-2.

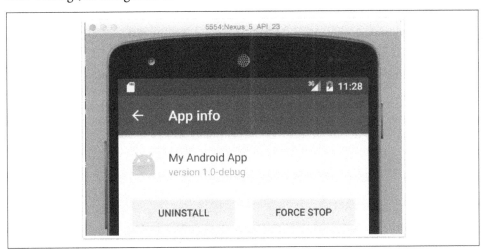

Figure 3-2. Version name in App info settings

Changing the name of the apps involves merging resources, discussed in Recipe 3.3. Different build types also allows you to create separate source trees for each. Merging sources from separate build types (and flavors) is discussed in Recipe 3.5.

See Also

Flavors are discussed in Recipe 3.2. The combination of a flavor and a build type is a variant. Each variant allows for separate resources, manifest entries, and Java source code, the merger of which is part of Recipes Recipe 3.3 and Recipe 3.5.

3.2 Product Flavors and Variants

Problem

You want to build essentially the same application, but with different resources and/or classes.

Solution

Product flavors allow you to create multiple different versions of the same app.

Discussion

Build types are part of the development process, normally used as an app evolves from development to production. The default build types, `debug` and `release`, reflect that.

Flavors allow you to build multiple versions of the same app. This could happen when you need to customize the look and feel of an app for different clients, or if you need both a free and a paid version of the same app.

To declare a product flavor, use the `productFlavors` block in the `android` closure.

Consider a "Hello, World" style of Android app that greets a user based on a simple `EditText` name entry. You can give the app an attitude by introducing "friendly," "arrogant," and "obsequious" flavors, as in Example 3-4.

Example 3-4. Assigning product flavors

```
android {
    productFlavors {
        arrogant {
            applicationId 'com.oreilly.helloworld.arrg'
        }

        friendly {
            applicationId 'com.oreilly.helloworld.frnd'
```

```
        }
        obsequious {
            applicationId 'com.oreilly.helloworld.obsq'
        }
    }
}
```

In this case, each has a slightly different `applicationId`, so that all three can be installed on the same device.

 Flavor names can't match existing build type names or the predefined name `androidTest`.

Each product flavor can have its own values of the following properties, among others, which are based on the same properties from `defaultConfig`:

- `applicationId`
- `minSdkVersion`
- `targetSdkVersion`
- `versionCode`
- `versionName`
- `signingConfig`

Each flavor defines its own source set and resources, which are siblings of the main source set. For the flavors defined in Example 3-4, that means in addition to *app/src/main/java*, you can also add source files in:

- *app/src/arrogant/java*
- *app/src/friendly/java*
- *app/src/obsequious/java*

You can also add additional resource files in:

- *app/src/arrogant/res*
- *app/src/arrogant/res/layout*
- *app/src/arrogant/res/values*

as well as any other subdirectories of *res*. The same resource structure would also apply for all flavors. A simple example is shown in Figure 3-3.

A similar folder structure is supported for build types as well. The combination of a build type and a flavor is called a *variant*. For the two default build types (debug and release) and the three flavors shown here (arrogant, friendly, and obsequious), six different variant APKs can be generated.

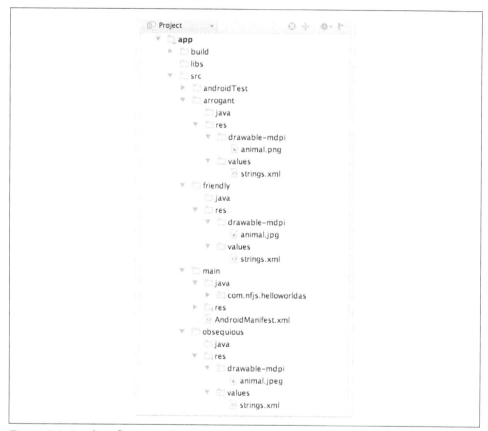

Figure 3-3. Product flavors with source code and resources

To see all the available variant names, add the custom task in Example 3-5 to your module build.

Example 3-5. A custom task to print available variants

```
task printVariantNames() {
    doLast {
        android.applicationVariants.all { variant ->
            println variant.name
```

```
        }
    }
}
```

Execution of the `printVariantNames` task shows them all, as in Example 3-6.

> Writing your own Gradle tasks is discussed in Recipe 4.1.

Example 3-6. Printing all the variant names

```
> ./gradlew printVariantNames
:app:printVariantNames
obsequiousDebug
obsequiousRelease
arrogantDebug
arrogantRelease
friendlyDebug
friendlyRelease

BUILD SUCCESSFUL
```

To deploy a particular variant, Android Studio provides a Build Variants view. Choose the proper variant from the dropdown list, as shown in Figure 3-4, and deploy as usual.

Figure 3-4. Build Variants view in Android Studio

When product flavors are used, the `assemble` task builds all possible variants. The `assemble<Variant>` task builds only that particular combination of build type and flavor. You can also run `assemble<BuildType>` to build all flavors in that build type, or `assemble<Flavor>` to build all build types for that flavor. The `install` tasks are specific to each variant, as in `installArrogantDebug` or `installFriendlyRelease`.

See Also

Merging resources from different flavors and build types is discussed in Recipe 3.3. Changing Java classes in each is discussed in Recipe 3.5. Writing your own custom tasks in Gradle is shown in Recipe 4.1.

3.3 Merging Resources

Problem

You want to change the images, text, or other resources in a product flavor.

Solution

Add the proper resource directories to your flavor, add the relevant files, and change the values they contain.

Discussion

Consider the "Hello World with Attitude" application discussed in Recipe 3.2, which defined three flavors for the Hello, World app: *arrogant*, *friendly*, and *obsequious*. In each case, the app prompts the user for a name and then greets the user by name. The Java code for each is identical, but the look and feel for each flavor is different.

The product flavors are defined in the Gradle build file, as shown in Example 3-7.

Example 3-7. Product flavors in the build.gradle file

```
android {
    // ... other settings ...

    productFlavors {
        arrogant {
            applicationId 'com.oreilly.helloworld.arrg'
        }
        friendly {
            applicationId 'com.oreilly.helloworld.frnd'
        }
        obsequious {
            applicationId 'com.oreilly.helloworld.obsq'
        }
    }
}
```

Each flavor is given a separate `applicationId` so that they can all be deployed to the same device for demonstration purposes.

Example 3-8 contains the MainActivity class, with its onCreate and sayHello methods.

Example 3-8. The MainActivity class from the Hello, World app

```
public class MainActivity extends AppCompatActivity {
    private EditText editText;

    @Override
    protected void onCreate(Bundle savedInstanceState) {
        super.onCreate(savedInstanceState);
        setContentView(R.layout.activity_main);

        editText = (EditText) findViewById(R.id.name_edit_text);
    }

    public void sayHello(View view) {
        String name = editText.getText().toString();
        Intent intent = new Intent(this, WelcomeActivity.class);
        intent.putExtra("user", name);
        startActivity(intent);
    }
}
```

The activity has an attribute of type EditText, used for the user's name. The say Hello method retrieves the name, adds it to an Intent as an extra, and starts the WelcomeActivity with the intent.

The layout for the main activity is simply a vertical LinearLayout with a TextView, an EditText, and a Button (Example 3-9).

Example 3-9. The activity_main.xml layout

```
<LinearLayout xmlns:android="http://schemas.android.com/apk/res/android"
    xmlns:tools="http://schemas.android.com/tools"
    android:layout_width="match_parent"
    android:layout_height="match_parent"
    android:orientation="vertical"
    tools:context=".MainActivity">

    <TextView
        android:id="@+id/name_text_view"
        android:layout_width="wrap_content"
        android:layout_height="wrap_content"
        android:text="@string/hello_world" />

    <EditText
        android:id="@+id/name_edit_text"
        android:hint="@string/name_hint"
        android:layout_width="match_parent"
```

```
        android:layout_height="wrap_content" />

    <Button
        android:onClick="sayHello"
        android:text="@string/hello_button_label"
        android:layout_width="wrap_content"
        android:layout_height="wrap_content" />

</LinearLayout>
```

The MainActivity is the launcher. Figure 3-5 shows the initial screen for the application, customized for the arrogant flavor.

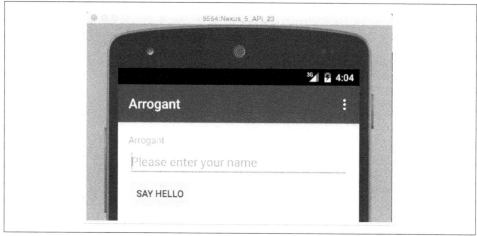

Figure 3-5. Hello screen in the Arrogant flavor

How were the application name and initial greeting set? All three flavors have their own resources directory, under *app/<flavor>/res*. In each case, a subfolder called *values* was added, and a copy of the *strings.xml* file from *app/src/main/res/values* was copied into it. The project structure for the arrogant flavor is shown in Figure 3-6.

The *strings.xml* file for the arrogant flavor is shown in Example 3-10.

Example 3-10. The strings.xml file in the Arrogant res/values folder

```
<resources>
    <string name="app_name">Arrogant</string>
    <string name="title_activity_welcome">His/Her Royal Highness</string>
    <string name="hello_world">Arrogant</string>
    <string name="greeting">We condescend to acknoweldge your
        presence, if just barely, %1$s.</string>
</resources>
```

Figure 3-6. Project view showing Arrogant flavor directories

Merging resources by combining the values in the *res* folder of the project flavor with the same folder from a build type and the main directory tree. The priority is: build type overrides Product Flavor, which overrides the main source set.

Non-Java resources override each other, where build type has highest priority, then flavor, then the main directory.

The WelcomeActivity has an onCreate method that retrieves the user's name and greets the user (Example 3-11).

Example 3-11. The WelcomeActivity, which greets the user

```java
public class WelcomeActivity extends AppCompatActivity {

    @Override
    protected void onCreate(Bundle savedInstanceState) {
        super.onCreate(savedInstanceState);
        setContentView(R.layout.activity_welcome);

        String name = getIntent().getStringExtra("user");
        TextView greetingText = (TextView) findViewById(R.id.greeting_text);
        String format = getString(R.string.greeting);
        greetingText.setText(String.format(format, name));
    }
}
```

The layout for the WelcomeActivity consists of a TextView with text and an image at the bottom (Example 3-12).

Example 3-12. The activity_welcome.xml layout

```xml
<LinearLayout xmlns:android="http://schemas.android.com/apk/res/android"
    xmlns:tools="http://schemas.android.com/tools"
    android:layout_width="match_parent"
    android:layout_height="match_parent"
    android:orientation="vertical"
    tools:context="com.oreilly.helloworld.WelcomeActivity">

    <TextView
        android:id="@+id/greeting_text"
        android:layout_width="wrap_content"
        android:layout_height="wrap_content"
        android:text="@string/hello_world"
        android:textSize="24sp"
        android:drawableBottom="@drawable/animal"
        />

</LinearLayout>
```

Each flavor has its own *values.xml* and *animal.png* files, which change the greeting given. The values in Example 3-10 result in the welcome shown in Figure 3-7.

Each additional flavor is handled the same way. The `friendly` flavor uses the *strings.xml* file shown in Example 3-13.

Example 3-13. The strings.xml file in the Friendly res/values folder

```xml
<resources>
    <string name="app_name">Friendly</string>
    <string name="title_activity_welcome">We are BFFs!</string>
    <string name="hello_world">Friendly</string>
    <string name="greeting">Hi there, %1$s!</string>
</resources>
```

The Friendly welcome page is shown in Figure 3-8.

Finally, the Obsequious strings are shown in Example 3-14.

Example 3-14. The strings.xml file in the Obsequious res/values folder

```xml
<resources>
    <string name="app_name">Obsequious</string>
    <string name="hello_world">Obsequious</string>
    <string name="title_activity_welcome">your humble servant</string>
    <string name="greeting">O great %1$s, please accept this pathetic
        greeting from my unworthy self. I grovel in your
        general direction.</string>
</resources>
```

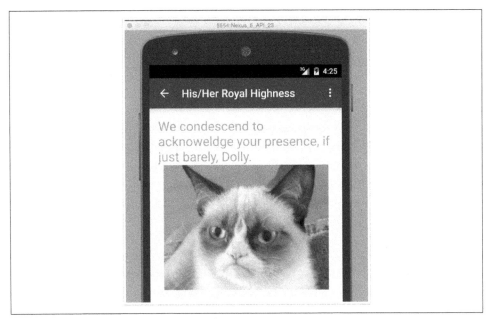

Figure 3-7. Welcome in the Arrogant flavor

Figure 3-8. Welcome in the friendly flavor

The resulting Obsequious welcome page is shown in Figure 3-9.

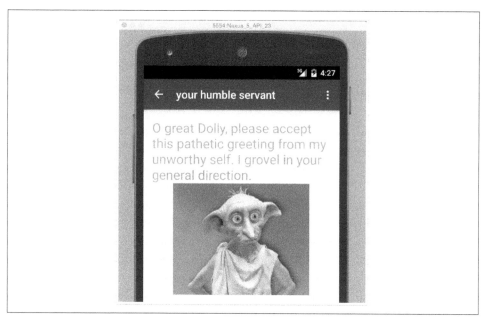

Figure 3-9. Welcome in the Obsequious flavor

Merging non-Java resources is easy. Just add the proper folders and files, and the flavor values will override those from main. To deploy an individual flavor of the app, choose it from the Build Variants view, as in Figure 3-10.

Figure 3-10. Build Variants view in Android Studio

See Also

Flavors and variants are discussed in Recipe 3.2. Merging source code is in Recipe 3.5.

3.4 Flavor Dimensions

Problem

One product flavor is not enough. You need another criterion to distinguish different versions of your app.

Solution

Add `flavorDimensions` to your product flavors.

Discussion

The recipe in Recipe 3.2 showed a "Hello, World" app with three product flavors: `arrogant`, `friendly`, and `obsequious`. That means the different flavors are being distinguished based on attitude.

Suppose, however, that different clients would like their own branded versions of each flavor of the app. The source code is essentially the same for each. Only a couple of minor resources are different.

To keep from having too much duplication, introduce an additional flavor dimension. The build file is shown in Example 3-15.

Example 3-15. Adding flavor dimensions

```
flavorDimensions 'attitude', 'client'

productFlavors {
    arrogant {
        dimension 'attitude'
        applicationId 'com.oreilly.helloworld.arrg'
    }
    friendly {
        dimension 'attitude'
        applicationId 'com.oreilly.helloworld.frnd'
    }
    obsequious {
        dimension 'attitude'
        applicationId 'com.oreilly.helloworld.obsq'
    }
    stark {
        dimension 'client'
    }
    wayne {
        dimension 'client'
    }
}
```

There are now two dimensions of flavor: attitude and client. The arrogant, friendly, and obsequious flavors are all in the attitude dimension, and the stark and wayne flavors are types of client.

The combination generates many more variants. Running the printVariantNames custom task from Recipe 4.1 now shows the results in Example 3-16.

Example 3-16. Printing all the variant names

```
./gradlew printVariantNames
:app:printVariantNames
obsequiousStarkDebug
obsequiousStarkRelease
obsequiousWayneDebug
obsequiousWayneRelease
arrogantStarkDebug
arrogantStarkRelease
arrogantWayneDebug
arrogantWayneRelease
friendlyStarkDebug
friendlyStarkRelease
friendlyWayneDebug
friendlyWayneRelease

BUILD SUCCESSFUL
```

The combination of two build types with three attitudes and two clients gives 2 * 3 * 2 = 12 different variants.

To make the client variant actually do something visible, add directory trees for each of the client flavors, as in Figure 3-11.

The *colors.xml* file in the stark client *res/values* folder is in Example 3-17.

Example 3-17. The colors.xml file in the stark/res/values folder

```xml
<?xml version="1.0" encoding="utf-8"?>
<resources>
    <color name="text_color">#beba46</color>
    <color name="background_color">#771414</color>
</resources>
```

The corresponding *colors.xml* file in the *wayne/res/values* folder is shown in Example 3-18.

Example 3-18. The colors.xml file in the wayne/res/values folder

```xml
<?xml version="1.0" encoding="utf-8"?>
<resources>
```

```
    <color name="text_color">#beba46</color>
    <color name="background_color">#771414</color>
</resources>
```

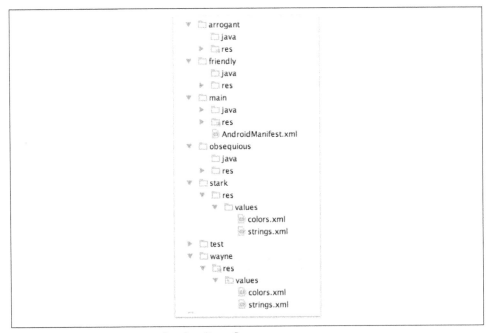

Figure 3-11. Directory trees for the client flavors

The *strings.xml* file in each client flavor changes just the `hello_world` string (Examples 3-19 and 3-20).

Example 3-19. The strings.xml file in the stark/res/values folder

```
<resources>
    <string name="hello_world">Stark Industries</string>
</resources>
```

Example 3-20. The strings.xml file in the wayne/res/values folder

```
<resources>
    <string name="hello_world">Wayne Enterprises</string>
</resources>
```

Finally, the `TextView` in the *activity_main.xml* layout file has been modified to use the new colors and strings (Example 3-21).

Example 3-21. Updated TextView element with colors and text

```
<TextView
    android:id="@+id/name_text_view"
    android:layout_width="match_parent"
    android:layout_height="wrap_content"
    android:textColor="@color/text_color"
    android:background="@color/background_color"
    android:textSize="32sp"
    android:text="@string/hello_world" />
```

The `textColor` attribute uses the color resource for each flavor, and the `text` attribute uses the string value provided by each flavor.

As a result, Figure 3-12 shows the `arrogant` flavor from Stark Industries.

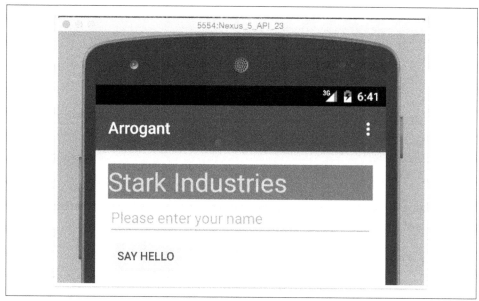

Figure 3-12. The Arrogant debug flavor from Stark Industries

By contrast, the `friendly` flavor from Wayne Enterprises is shown in Figure 3-13.

One additional note is necessary here. The `flavorDimensions` tag in the Gradle build file listed `attitude` before `client`, which means values from the attitude dimension will have higher priority than the client dimension. Therefore, the `hello_world` string resource was removed from each of the attitude flavors. Switching the order of `client` and `attitude` would have worked just as well, of course.

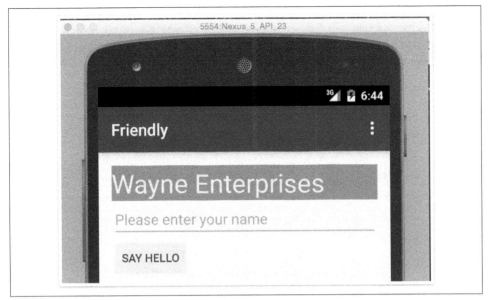

Figure 3-13. The Friendly debug flavor from Wayne Enterprises

See Also

Flavors and variants are shown in Recipe 3.2. Resource merging is in Recipe 3.3, and merging Java source code is in Recipe 3.5. Build types are discussed in Recipe 3.1.

3.5 Merging Java Sources Across Flavors

Problem

You want to add Android activities or other Java classes to individual product flavors.

Solution

Create the proper source folders, add your Java classes, and merge them with the main source set.

Discussion

While string and layout resources in flavors and build types override the corresponding values in the main source set, Java classes are different. If your code in the main source set refers to a particular class, then each flavor and build type can have its own implementation of that class as long as you don't have one in main.

That sounds more complicated than it is. The "Hello, World" app discussed in Recipe 3.2 and Recipe 3.4 has two flavors that represent clients. Consider now a modified version of that app that adds a button to the main activity to call for help. The additional button has the label "Call for Help!"

The main (launch) activity for the friendly, wayne flavor is shown in Figure 3-14.

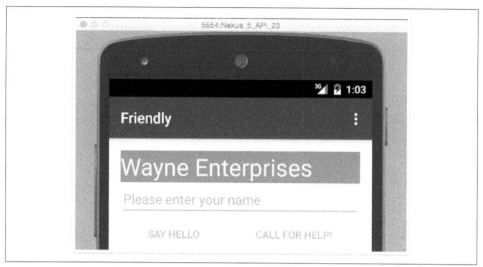

Figure 3-14. Main activity for the "wayne" client

The "stark" page is the same, just with a different header, as shown in Figure 3-15.

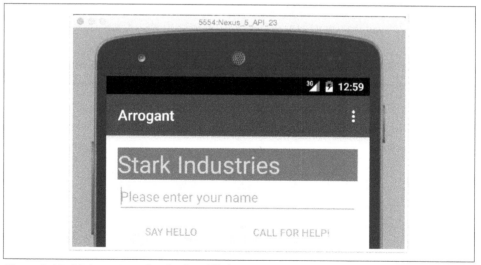

Figure 3-15. Main activity for the "stark" client

Clicking the "Call for Help!" button creates an `Intent` that starts the `CallForHelpAc` `tivity`. This activity, and its associated layout, have been removed from the `main` source tree, and a copy was added to both the `stark` and `wayne` source sets. The overall project layout when working with the `friendly`, `wayne`, `debug` variant is shown in Figure 3-16.

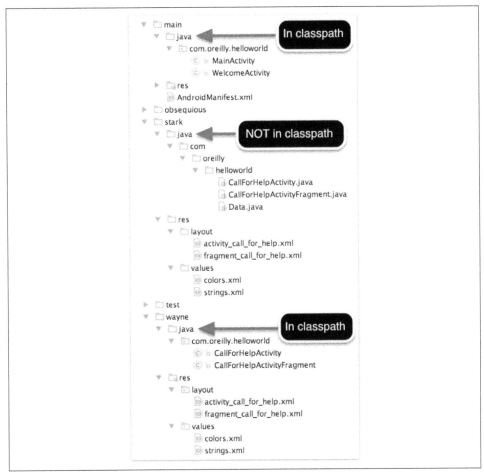

Figure 3-16. Source folders for main, stark, and wayne flavors

The figure shows that the Java sources in the `wayne` flavor are currently in the classpath and those in the `stark` tree are not. Both flavors contain the `CallForHelpActiv` `ity`, but the implementations of each are completely different.

For the `wayne` flavor, the help screen contains just a single fragment containing a `Text` `View`, as shown in Figure 3-17.

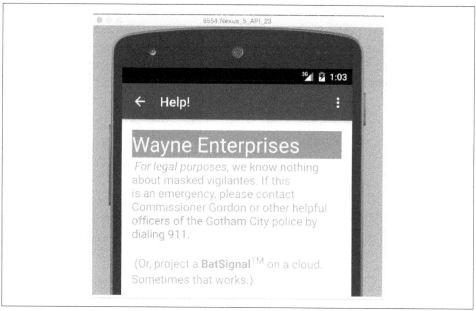

Figure 3-17. Help activity for wayne flavor

The help page for the `stark` flavor consists of a `ListFragment` with several entries, shown in Figure 3-18.

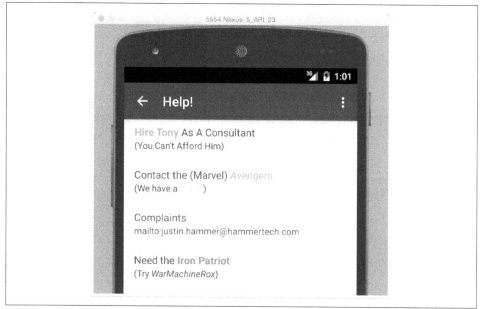

Figure 3-18. Help activity for stark flavor

Any class referenced by an element in the main source set must exist in each flavor. After that, the implementations are completely independent.

See Also

Recipe 3.2 shows how to implement flavors and variants. Recipe 3.3 is about merging non-Java resources. Recipe 3.4 shows how to have multiple flavor dimensions.

CHAPTER 4

Custom Tasks

4.1 Writing Your Own Custom Tasks

Problem

You want to customize the Gradle build process with your own tasks.

Solution

Add `task` elements to the Gradle build files. Use the extra properties supplied with the Android plug-in to make development easier.

Discussion

The Gradle DSL supports a `task` block for defining your own custom tasks. The API includes a wide range of existing tasks (like `Copy`, `Wrapper`, and `Exec`) that you can use simply by setting properties.

For example, the `Copy` task includes `from` and `into` properties, and the `from` block can be configured to exclude specified filename patterns. To copy all the APKs into a new folder, excluding those that are either unsigned or unaligned, add the task in Example 4-1 to the module build.

Example 4-1. Copy APKs to another folder

```
task copyApks(type: Copy) {
    from("$buildDir/outputs/apk") {
        exclude '**/*unsigned.apk', '**/*unaligned.apk'
    }
    into '../apks'
}
```

The buildDir property refers to the default build directory (*app/build*), and the dollar sign is used to inject it into a Groovy string (with double quotes). The documentation for the Copy task shows that the exclude block inside from supports an Ant-style directory name, meaning that ** matches all descendent directories.

If you don't want to simply configure an existing Gradle task, you need to understand the distinction between the *configuration* and *execution* phases of Gradle. During the configuration phase, Gradle builds a DAG based on their dependencies. It then executes the desired task, along with its dependencies. All tasks are configured before any are executed.

Gradle prefers declarative tasks, like the Example 4-1 task, where you specify what you want done but not how to do it. If you need to execute commands, however, add a doLast block to your Gradle task.

The task shown in Example 4-2, from Recipe 3.2, is repeated here.

Example 4-2. A custom task to print available variants

```
task printVariantNames() {
    doLast {
        android.applicationVariants.all { variant ->
            println variant.name
        }
    }
}
```

Anything done in the task either before or after the doLast block would be run during configuration time. The code in the doLast block itself runs at execution time.

The Android plug-in adds an android property, which in turn has an applica tionVariants property that returns all the buildType/flavor combinations. In this case, they are all being printed to the console.

 The applicationVariants property is only available for the com.android.application plug-in. A libraryVariants property is available in Android libraries. A testVariants property is available in both.

To install all the debug flavors onto a single device (assuming they all have unique applicationId values), use the task in Example 4-3.

Example 4-3. Install all the debug flavors on a single device

```
task installDebugFlavors() {
    android.applicationVariants.all { v ->
        if (v.name.endsWith('Debug')) {
            String name = v.name.capitalize()
            dependsOn "install$name"
        }
    }
}
```

In this case, the dependsOn method shows that this is part of the configuration process rather than execution. Each variant name, like friendlyDebug, is capitalized (FriendlyDebug) and then the corresponding installation task (install FriendlyDebug) is added as a dependency to the installDebugFlavors task.

The result is during the configuration process, installArrogantDebug, install FriendlyDebug, and installObsequiousDebug are all added as dependencies to installDebugFlavors. Therefore, executing installDebugFlavors at the command line requires all three flavor installs.

Example 4-4. Installing all the debug flavors

```
./gradlew instDebFl
:app:preBuild UP-TO-DATE
:app:preArrogantDebugBuild UP-TO-DATE
:app:checkArrogantDebugManifest
// ... lots of tasks ...
:app:assembleArrogantDebug UP-TO-DATE
:app:installArrogantDebug
Installing APK 'app-arrogant-debug.apk' on 'Nexus_5_API_23(AVD) - 6.0'
Installed on 1 device.
:app:checkFriendlyDebugManifest
// ... lots of tasks ...
:app:assembleFriendlyDebug UP-TO-DATE
:app:installFriendlyDebug
Installing APK 'app-friendly-debug.apk' on 'Nexus_5_API_23(AVD) - 6.0'
Installed on 1 device.
:app:checkObsequiousDebugManifest
// ... lots of tasks ...
:app:assembleObsequiousDebug UP-TO-DATE
:app:installObsequiousDebug
Installing APK 'app-obsequious-debug.apk' on 'Nexus_5_API_23(AVD) - 6.0'
Installed on 1 device.
:app:installDebugFlavors

BUILD SUCCESSFUL
```

Extending the ADP Timeout Period

As an aside, while the build process is relatively quick, the deployment process may not be. The `android` tag supports an `adbOptions` tag to increase the amount of time allowed before the process hits a timeout limit (Example 4-5).

Example 4-5. Changing the ADB timeout period

```
android {
    adbOptions {
        timeOutInMs = 30 * 1000
    }
}
```

This extends the timeout limit to 30 seconds. Adjust this value if you are getting `ShellCommandUnresponsiveException` failures.

You can see that writing your own custom tasks requires at least some knowledge of Groovy. An extensive discussion is therefore a bit beyond the scope of this book, but there are several good Groovy resources available. Additional Groovy concepts are defined in this book as they occur.

See Also

The Gradle plug-in User Guide (see Recipe 6.2) shows available properties in the `android` object. The documentation for the `Copy`, `Zip`, or other Gradle tasks is found on the Gradle website. Appendix A and Appendix B have background information on the Groovy programming language and basic Gradle information, respectively.

4.2 Adding Custom Tasks to the Build Process

Problem

You want to call your custom tasks as part of an overall build process.

Solution

Use the `dependOn` property to insert your task into the directed acyclic graph.

Discussion

During the initialization phase, Gradle assembles the tasks into a sequence according to their dependencies. The result is a DAG. For example, the Gradle documentation forms a DAG for the Java plug-in, as shown in Figure 4-1.

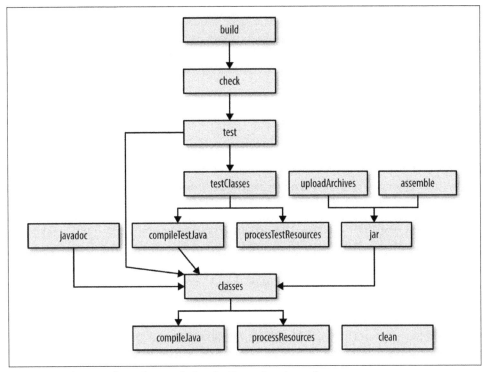

Figure 4-1. Directed acyclic graph for the Java plug-in tasks

The "directed" term means each dependency arrow goes in one direction. "Acyclic" means that there are no loops in the graph.

Adding your own custom task to the process means inserting your task into the graph at the proper location.

In Recipe 4.1, the copyApks task was defined to copy all the generated APKs into a separate directory. That task is reproduced in Example 4-6 for convenience.

Example 4-6. Copy APKs to another folder

```
task copyApks(type: Copy) {
    from("$buildDir/outputs/apk") {
        exclude '**/*unsigned.apk', '**/*unaligned.apk'
    }
    into '../apks'
}
```

That task isn't very useful, however, if the APKs have not yet been generated. The assemble task builds the APKs, so make it a dependency of the copyApks task, as in Example 4-7.

Example 4-7. Updated copy task to generate them first

```
task copyApks(type: Copy, dependsOn: assembleDebug) { ❶
    from("$buildDir/outputs/apk") {
        exclude '**/*unsigned.apk', '**/*unaligned.apk'
    }
    into '../apks'
}
```

❶ Run `assembleDebug` first

The dependency on `assembleDebug` means all the debug APKs will be generated before the copy task runs. You can use `assemble` instead if you want the release APKs as well.

If you would like the `copyApks` task to run every time you do a build, make it a dependency of the `build` task, as in Example 4-8.

Example 4-8. Making copyApks a part of the build

```
build.dependsOn copyApks
```

Now running the `build` task will also copy the APKs into the separate folder. You have inserted the `copyApks` task into the DAG with the correct dependency information.

Removing the generated *apks* folder containing all the APKs can be done in a similar fashion, but as shown in Recipe 1.1, the top-level Gradle build file already has a `clean` task that we can modify, as shown in Example 4-9.

Example 4-9. clean task generated by Android Studio

```
task clean(type: Delete) {
    delete rootProject.buildDir
}
```

The `delete` task in Gradle accepts a list of files or folders, so rather than make a special task to remove the *apks* folder, it's easy enough to modify this task, as shown in Example 4-10.

Example 4-10. Modified clean task to remove the apks directory

```
task clean(type: Delete) {
    delete rootProject.buildDir, 'apks'
}
```

Any custom task can be inserted into the build process using this mechanism.

See Also

Recipe 4.1 discusses creating custom tasks in Android builds. The topic of custom tasks is part of Appendix B.

4.3 Excluding Tasks

Problem

You want to exclude certain tasks from the build process.

Solution

Exclude an individual task using the -x flag. Exclude multiple tasks by modifying the task graph.

Discussion

The Gradle build process involves a lot of tasks executed sequentially. Most of them depend on tasks executed earlier in the process, but there are some that can be excluded if time is critical.

As an example, the lint task is useful for determining how closely your project adheres to Google's recommended practices for Android apps, but you don't necessarily have to run it every time.

Recall that the -x flag (short for --exclude-task) in Gradle excludes a given task. Therefore, when running a build, use the flag to skip the lint task (or any others you don't want), as shown in Example 4-11.

Example 4-11. Excluding the lint task

```
> ./gradlew build -x lint
```

This excludes the lint task and any of its dependencies. Any task that need its result will not run either, so be sure that any task you exclude is not required later in the process.

The only problem is that if your project involves multiple variants, there is a lint task for each. In principle you could exclude them all manually, but you might prefer to exclude the whole set as part of the build.

When Gradle runs, it assembles a directed acyclic graph, known as a *task graph*. You can get a reference to it inside your build file through the gradle object. Any manipulation of the graph needs to be done after it has been formed, so you want to use the whenReady property before applying any changes.

The result is you can write code inside the build file like that shown in Example 4-12.

Example 4-12. Disabling all tasks that start with the word lint

```
gradle.taskGraph.whenReady { graph ->
    graph.allTasks.findAll { it.name ==~ /lint.*/ }*.enabled = false
}
```

The `allTasks` property of the task graph invokes the `getAllTasks` method, using the normal Groovy idiom. That returns a `java.util.List` of tasks. Groovy adds a `findAll` method to `List` that returns only the tasks that satisfy the supplied closure. In this case, the closure says access the `name` property of each task and check whether or not it exactly matches the regular expression. Applying the "spread-dot" operator to the resulting list disables each task in the list.

The result is that all tasks that have a name that starts with the letters `lint` have their `enabled` property set to `false`, so none of them will run.

Since you may not want to always exclude all the `lint` tasks, you can check whether or not a project property has been set before doing this, as in Example 4-13.

Example 4-13. Only disable the lint tasks if the noLint property is set

```
gradle.taskGraph.whenReady { graph ->
    if (project.hasProperty('noLint')) {
        graph.allTasks.findAll { it.name ==~ /lint.*/ }*.enabled = false
    }
}
```

You can set a project property from the command line using the `-P` flag, as in Example 4-14.

Example 4-14. Setting a project property

```
> ./gradlew build -PnoLint | grep lint
:app:lintVitalArrogantRelease SKIPPED
:app:lintVitalFriendlyRelease SKIPPED
:app:lintVitalObsequiousRelease SKIPPED
:app:lint SKIPPED
```

Clearly there's a fair amount of Groovy knowledge involved in this approach, but the idea of manipulating the task graph after it has been assembled is a very powerful one.

See Also

Recipe 2.1 discusses how to set project properties. Excluding tasks as a means of improving build performance is part of Recipe 6.1.

4.4 Custom Source Sets

Problem

You want to use nonstandard directories for source code in your project.

Solution

Use the sourceSets property in your Gradle build.

Discussion

The samples that come with the Android distribution are configured to use multiple source folders, in order to separate common files from the main sample code.

Consider an arbitrary example from the API 23 (Android 6.0, Marshmallow) distribution, called Basic Gesture Detect, which is found in the *input/BasicGestureDetect* folder of the samples section. The details of the application itself are not important—it's the Gradle build that shows the source set modifications.

Example 4-15 shows the Gradle build file from the *Application* subdirectory (note that the samples commonly use Application instead of app for the main subproject).

Example 4-15. Gradle build file with source sets

```
// The sample build uses multiple directories to
// keep boilerplate and common code separate from
// the main sample code.
List<String> dirs = [
    'main',     // main sample code; look here for the interesting stuff.
    'common',   // components that are reused by multiple samples
    'template'] // boilerplate code that is generated by the sample template process

android {
    // ... code omitted ...

    sourceSets {
        main {
            dirs.each { dir ->
                java.srcDirs "src/${dir}/java"
                res.srcDirs "src/${dir}/res"
            }
        }
```

```
        androidTest.setRoot('tests')
        androidTest.java.srcDirs = ['tests/src']

    }

}
```

The build file defines a `List<String>` called `dirs` to represent the source directories. Groovy supports a native syntax for lists, using square brackets with values separated by commas. In this case, the values are `main`, `common`, and `template`.

Inside the `android` block, the `sourceSets` property is used to add the relevant source directories to the classpath. Focusing on the section inside the `main` block, Groovy's `each` iterator supplies each entry in the list to the closure argument in Example 4-16.

Example 4-16. Groovy each with a closure

```
dirs.each { dir ->
    java.srcDirs "src/${dir}/java"
    res.srcDirs "src/${dir}/res"
}
```

The `each` method comes from Groovy. It iterates over every element of a collection, passing it into the closure argument. The closure here labels each element as `dir` and substitutes it into the Groovy strings.

The standard project layout defines a default source tree *src/main/java* and a resource tree *src/main/res*. In this case, however, additional directories are added to those collections by using the `srcDirs` property. The result in this case is that the folders *src/main/java*, *src/common/java*, and *src/template/java* are all added to the compile classpath, and the folders *src/main/res*, *src/common/res*, and *src/template/res* are all considered resource directories.

The real irony, however, is that this particular sample doesn't have any of the additional folders in it. All the Java sources are under *src/main/java* and all the resources are under *src/main/res*. In fact, none of the samples actually use the defined structure. They all restrict their Java source code and resources to the standard directories. The structure just defined is therefore either something planned for the future, or a holdover from something older, or maybe just evidence that the Google Android developers have a sense of humor.

There is one section of the `sourceSets` property that is used, however. Instead of putting all the tests under the predefined *src/androidTest/java* folder, the Gradle build file changes that location (Example 4-17).

Example 4-17. Changing the root directory for tests

```
androidTest.setRoot('tests')
androidTest.java.srcDirs = ['tests/src']
```

The test root is now the *tests* folder, and the tests themselves are placed in the *tests/src* folder. Each sample project has two folders underneath the *Application* directory: *src* and *tests*, and the *tests* folder contains a subdirectory called *src*. The basic project layout for the `ActivityInstrumentation` example contains an *Application* directory, whose contents are structured like that in Example 4-18.

Example 4-18. Directory layout for sample project

```
.
├── build.gradle
├── src
│   └── main
│       ├── AndroidManifest.xml
│       ├── java
│       │   └── com
│       │       └── example
│       │           └── android
│       │               ├── activityinstrumentation
│       │               │   └── MainActivity.java
│       │               ... // more
│       └── res
│           ├── drawable-hdpi
│           │   ├── ic_launcher.png
│           │   └── tile.9.png
│           ... // more
│           ├── values-v11
│           │   └── template-styles.xml
│           └── values-v21
│               ├── base-colors.xml
│               └── base-template-styles.xml
└── tests
    ├── AndroidManifest.xml
    └── src
        └── com
            └── example
                └── android
                    └── activityinstrumentation
                        └── SampleTests.java
```

As you can see, the Java code goes under *src/main/java*, the resources go under *src/main/res*, and the tests go under *tests/src* of all places.

Where does the `sourceSets` property get used? Legacy Android apps (e.g., those written before the conversion to the Gradle build system) used a different project structure. Android Studio can import those apps, but it will rewrite the structure when doing so. See Recipe 2.2 and Recipe 2.3 for details.

See Also

The `sourceSets` property is often used with legacy apps.

4.5 Using Android Libraries

Problem

You want to add library modules to your app.

Solution

Use the `library` plug-in and add the library module as a dependency.

Discussion

You can add a lot of additional functionality to an app by using Java libraries, which come in the form of `jar` files. Recipe 1.5 discusses this in detail, showing how to use the `dependencies` block. For example, to use Google's Gson library for parsing JSON data, add the dependency to the module build file, as shown in Example 4-19.

Example 4-19. Adding Google's Gson library

```
dependencies {
    compile 'com.google.code.gson:gson:2.6.2'
}
```

Android libraries go beyond Java libraries, in that they include either classes from the Android API, any needed resources, or both. When the project is built, Gradle assembles Android libraries into `aar` (Android Archive) files, which are like `jar` files but include the Android dependencies.

From a Gradle perspective, Android libraries are subprojects from the root. That means they are like Android applications, but in a subdirectory. The name of the added module (Android Studio calls them modules) is therefore added to the *settings.gradle* file, as in Example 4-20.

Example 4-20. A settings.gradle file with an added module

```
include ':app', ':icndb'
```

In this case, the Android library module is called `icndb`, which stands for the Internet Chuck Norris Database (*http://www.icndb.com*), which serves up Chuck Norris jokes in the form of JSON responses. The API page on the website is shown in Figure 4-2.

Figure 4-2. The API page for the ICNDB site

As an example of an Android library, this site will be accessed as a RESTful web service, the returned JSON data will be parsed, and the resulting joke will be added to the Welcome activity in a `TextView`.

To create a library module in Android Studio, use the "New Module" wizard and select the "Android Library" type, as in Figure 4-3.

Other options on the New Module wizard include Java Library and Import .JAR/.AAR Package, among others.

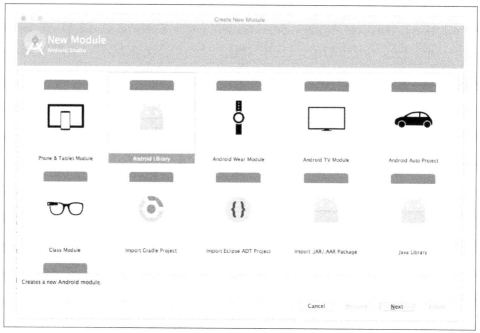

Figure 4-3. The Android Library option in the New Module wizard

After giving the library a name, you can then add whatever type of activity you want, if any. Completing the wizard creates the library directory and adds it to the *settings.gradle* file in the root project.

Each library has its own Gradle build file, which supports the same settings as the root project. You can specify minimum and target SDK versions, customize build types, add flavors, and modify dependencies however you like. The important difference is that the Gradle build uses a different plug-in, as shown in Example 4-21.

Example 4-21. The build.gradle file for the ICNDB library module

```
apply plugin: 'com.android.library'    ❶

android {
    compileSdkVersion 23
    buildToolsVersion "23.0.3"

    packagingOptions {    ❷
        exclude 'META-INF/notice.txt'
        exclude 'META-INF/license.txt'
        exclude 'LICENSE.txt'
    }

    defaultConfig {
```

```
        minSdkVersion 16
        targetSdkVersion 23
        versionCode 1
        versionName "1.0"
    }
    buildTypes {
        release {
            minifyEnabled false
            proguardFiles getDefaultProguardFile('proguard-android.txt'),
                'proguard-rules.pro'
        }
    }
}

dependencies {
    compile 'com.google.code.gson:gson:2.6.2'
    compile 'com.squareup.retrofit2:retrofit:2.0.1'
    compile 'com.squareup.retrofit2:converter-gson:2.0.1'
}
```

❶ Use the library plug-in

❷ Exclude conflicting files from multiple dependencies

The build file adds the Retrofit 2 project as a dependency, and its Gson converter for the JSON messages, as well as the Gson library discussed earlier.

Note also the use of the `packagingOptions` block. That allows you to exclude files of the same name that appear in multiple dependencies.

If you use these libraries, the implementation of the ICNDB library becomes simple, as shown in Example 4-22.

Example 4-22. The JokeFinder class, which does all the work

```
public class JokeFinder {
    private TextView jokeView;
    private Retrofit retrofit;
    private AsyncTask<String, Void, String> task;

    public interface ICNDB {   ❶
        @GET("/jokes/random")
        Call<IcndbJoke> getJoke(@Query("firstName") String firstName,
                                @Query("lastName") String lastName,
                                @Query("limitTo") String limitTo);
    }

    public JokeFinder() {
        retrofit = new Retrofit.Builder()   ❷
            .baseUrl("http://api.icndb.com")
            .addConverterFactory(GsonConverterFactory.create())
```

```
            .build();
    }

    public void getJoke(TextView textView, String first, String last) {
        this.textView = textView;
        new JokeTask().execute(first, last);
    }

    private class JokeTask extends AsyncTask<String, Void, String> { ❸
        @Override
        protected String doInBackground(String... params) {
            ICNDB icndb = retrofit.create(ICNDB.class);
            Call<IcndbJoke> icndbJoke = icndb.getJoke(
                params[0], params[1], "[nerdy]");
            String joke = "";
            try {
                joke = icndbJoke.execute().body().getJoke();
            } catch (IOException e) {
                e.printStackTrace();
            }
            return joke;
        }

        @Override
        protected void onPostExecute(String result) {
            jokeView.setText(result);
        }
    }
}
```

❶ Interface for Retrofit GET request access

❷ Building the Retrofit instance with Gson converter

❸ Asynchronous task to access web service off the UI thread

The JokeFinder class accesses the ICNDB web service using the supplied first and last names for the hero, using an asynchronous task so that the operation is performed off the UI thread. The getJoke method includes an argument for a TextView, which the JokeTask updates once parsing of the result is complete.

The IcndbJoke task is a simple POJO that maps the the JSON response. The form of the response is shown in Figure 4-4.

The JSON response is quite small, so the corresponding IcndbJoke class is also simple, as shown in Example 4-23.

Example 4-23. The IcndbJoke class POJO, which maps to the JSON format

```java
public class IcndbJoke {
    private String type;
    private Joke value;

    public String getJoke() {
        return value.getJoke();
    }

    public String getType() { return type; }
    public void setType(String type) { this.type = type; }

    public Joke getValue() { return value; }
    public void setValue(Joke value) { this.value = value;}

    private static class Joke {
        private int ID;
        private String joke;
        private String[] categories;

        public int getId() { return ID; }
        public void setId(int ID) { this.id = ID; }

        public String getJoke() { return joke; }
        public void setJoke(String joke) { this.joke = joke; }

        public String[] getCategories() { return categories; }
        public void setCategories(String[] categories) {
            this.categories = categories;
        }
    }
}
```

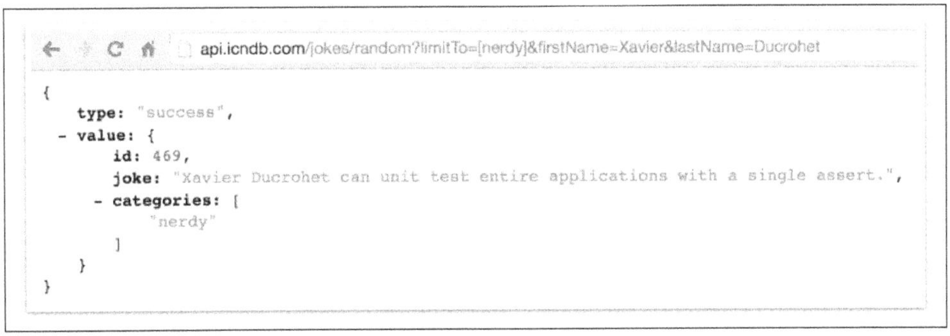

```
←  ⟳  C  ⌂     api.icndb.com/jokes/random?limitTo=[nerdy]&firstName=Xavier&lastName=Ducrohet

{
    type: "success",
  - value: {
        id: 469,
        joke: "Xavier Ducrohet can unit test entire applications with a single assert.",
      - categories: [
            "nerdy"
        ]
    }
}
```

Figure 4-4. JSON response from the ICNDB service

That's it for the library. The app uses the library through its JokeFinder class. This is
made available using a project dependency in the module build file, as shown in
Example 4-24.

Example 4-24. Using the ICNDB module in the app

```
apply plug-in: 'com.android.application'

android {
    compileSdkVersion 23
    buildToolsVersion "23.0.3"

    // ... all the regular settings ...
}

dependencies {
    compile project(':icndb')  ❶
}
```

❶   Use the `icndb` library at compile time

The `compile` dependency uses the `project` method, which takes the subdirectory containing the module as an argument. The result is that Gradle knows to build the ICNDB module before building the app, and to make its classes available at compile time.

The `WelcomeActivity` calls the `getJoke` method in the `JokeFinder`, supplying a reference to the `TextView` to be updated, along with a first and last name supplied from a `SharedPreferences` object, as seen in Example 4-25, where all the other parts have been omitted.

Example 4-25. Invoking the getJoke method from the WelcomeActivity

```
public class WelcomeActivity extends Activity {
    private TextView jokeText;

    @Override
    protected void onCreate(Bundle savedInstanceState) {
        super.onCreate(savedInstanceState);
        setContentView(R.layout.activity_welcome);

        jokeText = (TextView) findViewById(R.id.joke_text);

        final SharedPreferences prefs =
            PreferenceManager.getDefaultSharedPreferences(this);
        new JokeFinder().getJoke(jokeText,
                prefs.getString("first", "Xavier"),
                prefs.getString("last", "Ducrohet"));
    }
}
```

Xavier Ducrohet is the head of the Gradle plug-in for Android project and head of the Android Studio development team at Google.

A sample run is shown in Figure 4-5.

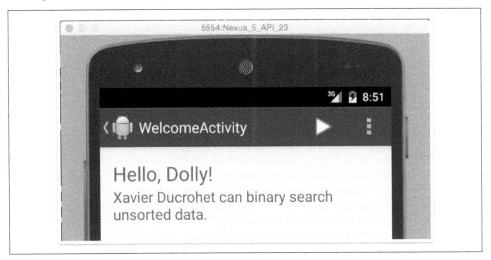

Figure 4-5. Running the app

The build process itself generates both debug and release versions of the library in the *icndb/build/outputs/arr* directory, shown in Example 4-26.

Example 4-26. Output Android library archive files

```
> ./gradlew build
> ls icndb/build/outputs/aar
icndb-debug.aar     icndb-release.aar
```

The `aar` files can be published to repositories for later use by other apps.

To summarize:

- Android library projects are Java projects that need Android dependencies, like classes from the Android API or resources or both
- Gradle uses subdirectories for multiproject builds, where each subproject is added to the top-level *settings.gradle* file
- In Android Studio, use the "Android Library" option in the "New Module" wizard to create an Android library project

- The library project uses the `com.android.library` plug-in
- The app build file uses the `project(":library")` dependency to access the library classes from the app

Following this pattern, you can add functionality to Android libraries and reuse them in other applications.

CHAPTER 5

Testing

5.1 Unit Testing

Problem

You want to test the non-Android parts of your app.

Solution

Use the experimental unit testing support added in version 1.1 of Android Studio and the Gradle plug-in for Android.

Discussion

The Eclipse Android Development Tools (ADT) plug-in only supported integration tests, and required developers to create a separate project just for the tests themselves. One of the advantages of the switch to Android Studio and Gradle was support for tests inside the Android project itself.

Prior to version 1.1 of Android Studio and the associated Gradle plug-in, however, those tests were still restricted to integration tests, meaning you needed either an emulator or a connected device in order to run the tests. Integration tests can be very powerful and useful, and are the subject of Recipes Recipe 5.3 and Recipe 5.4.

This recipe discusses true unit tests, which run on a local JVM on a development machine. Unlike the integration tests that use an `androidTest` source set, the unit tests reside in the *src/test/java* directory of your app.

When you generate a new Android app in Android Studio, a sample unit test is provided for you. It resides in the *src/test/java* tree, but is not currently in the classpath, as Figure 5-1 shows.

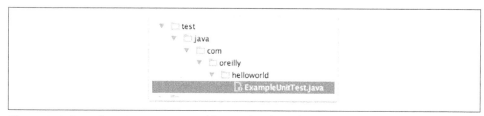

Figure 5-1. Sample unit test generated by Android Studio, under app/src

The generated test is shown in Example 5-1.

Example 5-1. Generated sample unit test

```java
import org.junit.Test;

import static org.junit.Assert.*;

/**
 * To work on unit tests, switch the Test Artifact in the Build Variants view.
 */
public class ExampleUnitTest {
    @Test
    public void addition_isCorrect() throws Exception {
        assertEquals(4, 2 + 2);
    }
}
```

This type of test should look familiar to anyone who has used JUnit in the past, which should be virtually every Java developer. The `@Test` annotation from JUnit 4 indicates that the `addition_isCorrect` method is a test method. The `assertEquals` method is a static method in the `Assert` class (note the static import of all static methods in that class), whose first argument is the correct answer and whose second argument is the actual test.

In order to run the test, you need to do what the comment says, which is to select the Test Artifact in the Build Variants view, as shown in Figure 5-2.

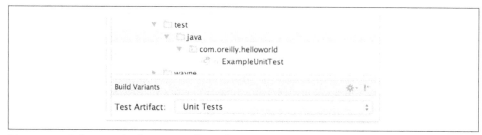

Figure 5-2. Selecting the "Unit Tests" artifact in Build Variants

Note that by selecting "Unit Tests," the directory tree under *src/test/java* is now understood by Android Studio to contain test sources (because the folder is shown in green) and the *com/oreilly/helloworld* tree is now interpreted as a package.

One last step is required before executing the unit test. You need to make sure JUnit is included as a `testCompile` dependency in your project. As shown in Recipe 1.5, this is already the case for the default project. The dependencies section of the module build file is repeated in Example 5-2.

Example 5-2. JUnit dependency in the module build.gradle file

```
dependencies {
    compile fileTree(dir: 'libs', include: ['*.jar'])
    testCompile 'junit:junit:4.12'  ❶
    compile 'com.android.support:appcompat-v7:23.0.1'
}
```

❶ JUnit dependency added during `testCompile`

You can now run the tests from Gradle using the `test` target, but be prepared for a lot of effort (see Example 5-3).

Example 5-3. Executing the unit test

```
> ./gradlew test
Starting a new Gradle Daemon for this build (subsequent builds will be faster).
:app:preBuild UP-TO-DATE
:app:preArrogantStarkDebugBuild UP-TO-DATE
:app:checkArrogantStarkDebugManifest
:app:preArrogantStarkReleaseBuild UP-TO-DATE
:app:preArrogantWayneDebugBuild UP-TO-DATE
:app:preArrogantWayneReleaseBuild UP-TO-DATE
:app:preFriendlyStarkDebugBuild UP-TO-DATE
:app:preFriendlyStarkReleaseBuild UP-TO-DATE
:app:preFriendlyWayneDebugBuild UP-TO-DATE
:app:preFriendlyWayneReleaseBuild UP-TO-DATE
// ... all the stages for all the variants ...
:app:compileObsequiousWayneReleaseUnitTestJavaWithJavac
:app:compileObsequiousWayneReleaseUnitTestSources
:app:assembleObsequiousWayneReleaseUnitTest
:app:testObsequiousWayneReleaseUnitTest
:app:test

BUILD SUCCESSFUL
```

The single test ran for every variant, generating HTML outputs in the *app/build/ reports/tests* folder, shown in Example 5-4.

Example 5-4. Output folders for the tests

```
> ls -F app/build/reports/tests/
arrogantStarkDebug/      arrogantWayneRelease/
friendlyWayneDebug/      obsequiousStarkRelease/
arrogantStarkRelease/    friendlyStarkDebug/
friendlyWayneRelease/    obsequiousWayneDebug/
arrogantWayneDebug/      friendlyStarkRelease/
obsequiousStarkDebug/    obsequiousWayneRelease/
```

Opening the *index.html* file in any of those folders shows the test report in Figure 5-3.

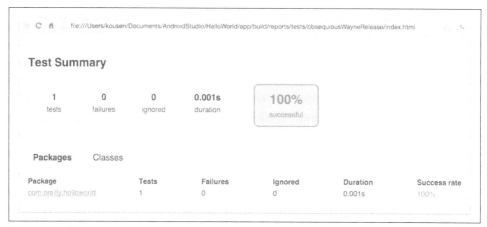

Figure 5-3. Test report in HTML

You can drill down to the ExampleUnitTest class and see the specific results (Figure 5-4).

To restrict the tests to a single variant and even a single test class, use the --tests flag, as in Example 5-5.

Example 5-5. Running the tests in only one test class

```
> ./gradlew testFriendlyWayneDebug --tests='*.ExampleUnitTest'
```

The variant is still constructed, but only that one, and only the tests in the Exam pleUnitTest class are run.

As an alternative, if you right-click in the test itself and run it inside Android Studio, it runs for the current variant only and provides a nice view showing the results (Figure 5-5).

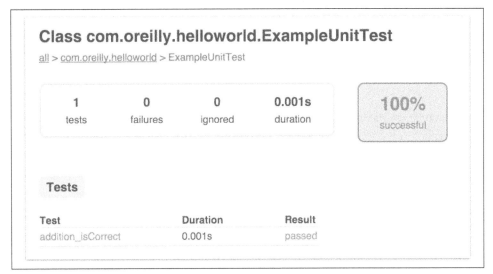

Class com.oreilly.helloworld.ExampleUnitTest

all > com.oreilly.helloworld > ExampleUnitTest

1	0	0	0.001s	100%
tests	failures	ignored	duration	successful

Tests

Test	Duration	Result
addition_isCorrect	0.001s	passed

Figure 5-4. Result of ExampleUnitTest tests

Figure 5-5. Test results in Android Studio

The only problem is, this didn't actually test anything significant. That's the point, actually. When using the JUnit support, you can't test anything that relies on the Android SDK. Unit testing is only for the purely Java parts of your application.

Unit testing support is only for the non-Android parts of your application.

In Recipe 4.5, the library accessed a web service, downloaded JSON data, parsed it, and updated a `TextView` with an included value. If you like, you can test just the parsing part of that process, as in Example 5-6.

Example 5-6. Test the Gson parser

```java
import com.google.gson.Gson;

import org.junit.Test;

import static org.junit.Assert.assertEquals;
import static org.junit.Assert.assertNotNull;

public class IcndbJokeTest {
    private String jsonTxt = "{\"type\": \"success\", \"value\": {\"id\": 451,
        \"joke\": \"Xav Ducrohet writes code that optimizes itself.\",
        \"categories\": [\"nerdy\"]}}";  ❶

    @Test
    public void testGetJoke() throws Exception {
        Gson gson = new Gson();
        IcndbJoke icndbJoke = gson.fromJson(jsonTxt, IcndbJoke.class);
        String correct = "Xav Ducrohet writes code that optimizes itself.";

        assertNotNull(icndbJoke);  ❷
        assertEquals(correct, icndbJoke.getJoke());  ❸
    }
}
```

❶   String should be all on one line

❷   Check that parsing yielded a non-null result

❸   Check that the retrieved joke is correct

The good news is that unit tests are fast, at least relative to integration tests, because they don't require deployment to an actual device or an emulator. If you have Java classes that are not dependent on Android classes, unit tests are great way to make sure they're working properly. Test Driven Development (TDD) has not yet been adopted in the mobile world the way it has in the regular Java world, but this is a good way to get started.

What About Robolectric?

The Robolectric project (*http://robolectric.org*) is designed to let you run integration tests as though they were unit tests, i.e., without using an emulator or connected device. As such, it acts as a giant mock of the entire Android SDK.

Reports from the field have been mixed. Some people really like it; others don't trust it for anything related to dialogs, animations, views, or anything else in the UI. This is

---

made more complicated by the fact you're scripting a UI test without actually using the UI.

Still, it's not a bad alternative, and fits into the overall Gradle approach. See the website for details.

See Also

Recipe 5.3 illustrates `Activity` tests using the Robotium library. Recipe 5.4 does the same using the Espresso framework from Google. JUnit information can be found at *http://junit.org*.

5.2 Testing with the Android Testing Support Library

Problem

You want to test the Android components of your app.

Solution

Use the new testing classes to implement JUnit-style tests of your app.

Discussion

First, a meta-note on terminology: testing Android components, like activities or services, requires deployment of the app to a connected device or emulator. The testing library is based on JUnit, but these are not unit tests in the strictest sense. They're either integration tests or functional tests, depending on how you use those terms.

Since the approach here is to drive a deployed app programmatically and check that the UI changes correctly, the term "functional" will be preferred here. You will see the term *integration* used frequently in the documentation, however.

Despite the word "unit" in `AndroidJUnitRunner` and other test classes, Android tests are inherently functional. They require either an emulator or a connected device in order to run.

The Android Testing Support Library is added as an optional dependency through the SDK Manager, as shown in Figure 5-6.

Testing is part of the "Android Support Repository" download, as Figure 5-6 illustrates. The testing classes reside in the `android.support.test` package.

The documentation shows that to add all the relevant classes to your Gradle build file, use the dependencies in Example 5-7.

Example 5-7. Gradle dependencies for the Android Testing Support Library

```
dependencies {
    androidTestCompile 'com.android.support.test:runner:0.3'
    // Set this dependency to use JUnit 4 rules
    androidTestCompile 'com.android.support.test:rules:0.3'
}
```

Figure 5-6. Adding the Android Testing Support Library using the SDK Manager

The AndroidJUnitRunner class has support for JUnit 4 annotations. To use it, you can add the @RunWith annotation from JUnit to your test class, or you can add a setting to the defaultConfig block of your Gradle build file.

Example 5-8. Using AndroidJUnitRunner by default

```
android {
    defaultConfig {
        // ... other settings ...
        testInstrumentationRunner
            "android.support.test.runner.AndroidJUnitRunner"
    }
}
```

It's particularly easy to test a labels on a layout using the test support classes. An example is shown in Example 5-9.

Example 5-9. Testing component labels

```
@MediumTest   ❶
@RunWith(AndroidJUnit4.class)   ❷
public class MyActivityLayoutTest
        extends ActivityInstrumentationTestCase2<MyActivity> {

    private MyActivity activity;
    private TextView textView;
```

```java
    private EditText editText;
    private Button helloButton;

    public MyActivityLayoutTest() {
        super(MyActivity.class);
    }

    @Before
    public void setUp() throws Exception {
        super.setUp()
        injectInstrumentation(InstrumentationRegistry.getInstrumentation());  ❸
        activity = getActivity();

        textView = (TextView) activity.findViewById(R.id.text_view);
        editText = (EditText) activity.findViewById(R.id.edit_text);
        helloButton = (Button) activity.findViewById(R.id.hello_button);
    }

    @After
    public void tearDown() throws Exception {
        super.tearDown();
    }

    @Test
    public void testPreconditions() {
        assertNotNull("Activity is null", activity);
        assertNotNull("TextView is null", textView);
        assertNotNull("EditText is null", editText);
        assertNotNull("HelloButton is null", helloButton);
    }

    @Test
    public void textView_label() {
        final String expected = activity.getString(R.string.hello_world);
        final String actual = textView.getText().toString();
        assertEquals(expected, actual);
    }

    @Test
    public void editText_hint() {
        final String expected = activity.getString(R.string.name_hint);
        final String actual = editText.getHint().toString();
        assertEquals(expected, actual);
    }

    @Test
    public void helloButton_label() {
        final String expected = activity.getString(R.string.hello_button_label);
        final String actual = helloButton.getText().toString();
        assertEquals(expected, actual);
    }
}
```

❶ Expected durations are @SmallTest, @MediumTest, and @LargeTest

❷ Use the JUnit 4 runner for Android

❸ Needed for the new JUnit 4 runner

The new `AndroidJUnitRunner` is part of the Android Support Test Library. It adds JUnit 4 support, so that tests can be annotated rather that specified using the old JUnit 3 naming convention. It has other extra capabilities. See the Android Testing Support Library documentation (*http://bit.ly/android-tsl*) for details.

In Example 5-9, the attributes represent widgets on the user interface. The `@Before` method looks them up and assigns them to the attributes. The docs recommend using a `testPreconditions` test like the one shown, just to demonstrate that the widgets were found. That test is no different from any of the others, but a failure there makes it easy to see what went wrong.

The other tests all look up strings from the string resources and compare them to the labels on the actual widgets. Note that nothing is being modified here—the test is essentially read-only.

Finally, the `@MediumTest` annotation is used to indicate the size of a test method. Tests that only take a few milliseconds are marked as `@SmallTest`, those that take on the order of 100 milliseconds are `@MediumTest`, and longer ones are marked `@LargeTest`.

From Gradle, running tests that require connected devices or emulators is done through the `connectedCheck` task.

 Run the `connectedCheck` task to execute tests on all emulators and connected devices concurrently.

A sample execution is shown in Example 5-10. The sample test was run concurrently on two separate emulators.

Example 5-10. Executing the tests from Gradle

```
> ./gradlew connectedCheck
:app:preBuild UP-TO-DATE
:app:preDebugBuild UP-TO-DATE
:app:checkDebugManifest
:app:prepareDebugDependencies
// ... lots of tasks ...
:app:packageDebugAndroidTest UP-TO-DATE
```

```
:app:assembleDebugAndroidTest UP-TO-DATE
:app:connectedDebugAndroidTest
:app:connectedAndroidTest
:app:connectedCheck

BUILD SUCCESSFUL
```

The output report resides in the *http://robolectric.orgapp/build/reports/androidTests/ connected* directory. A sample output report is shown in Figure 5-7.

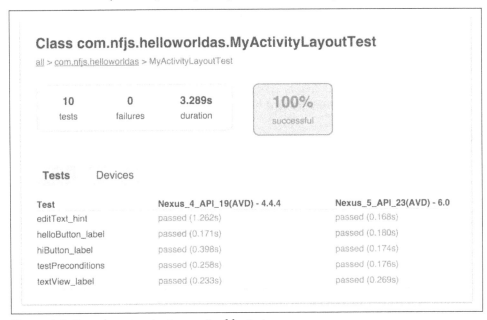

Figure 5-7. Sample test output organized by test

The sample output shows the emulator names and the results of all the tests. Clicking the "Devices" button switches the output to organize it by device, as shown in Figure 5-8.

The classes in the Android Support Test Library can do much more than this, but the tests start getting complicated quickly. When you want to drive the UI by adding data, clicking buttons, and checking results, there are alternative libraries, like Robotium and Espresso, that make the process much easier. Recipes that use those libraries are referenced in the "See Also" section.

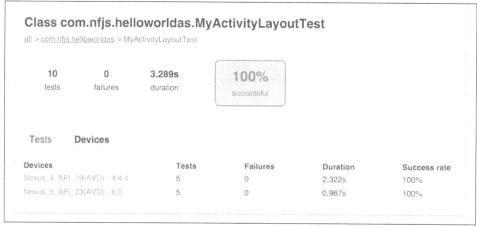

Class com.nfjs.helloworldas.MyActivityLayoutTest

all > com.nfjs.helloworldas > MyActivityLayoutTest

| 10 | 0 | 3.289s | 100% |
| tests | failures | duration | successful |

Tests   **Devices**

Devices	Tests	Failures	Duration	Success rate
Nexus_4_API_19(AVD) - 4.4.4	5	0	2.322s	100%
Nexus_5_API_23(AVD) - 6.0	5	0	0.967s	100%

Figure 5-8. Sample test output organized by device

See Also

Recipe 5.3 shows how to use the Robotium library to drive the UI. Google now provides the Espresso library as part of the Android Test Kit project. Espresso tests are demonstrated in Recipe 5.4.

5.3 Functional Testing with Robotium

Problem

You want to test activities using the Robotium library.

Solution

Add the Robotium dependency and script your tests.

Discussion

The Android Test Support Library has classes for accessing widgets on activities, but there are easier ways to drive an Android UI. While this is not a book about testing, it's easy to add the Robotium library dependency to Gradle and run tests that way.

The Robotium project (*http://www.robotium.org*) is described as "like Selenium, but for Android." It's a test automation framework that makes it easy to write black-box UI tests for Android apps.

Just add the Robotium library as a dependency in the module Gradle build file, as in Example 5-11.

Example 5-11. Add the Robotium dependency

```
dependencies {
    androidTestCompile 'com.jayway.android.robotium:robotium-solo:5.4.1'
}
```

Consider a simple activity called `MyActivity`, shown in Example 5-12, that prompts the user for a name, adds it to an `Intent`, and starts a `WelcomeActivity` that greets the user.

Example 5-12. The MyActivity class is a "Hello, World" app

```
public class MyActivity extends Activity {
    private TextView textView;
    private EditText editText;

    @Override
    protected void onCreate(Bundle savedInstanceState) {
        super.onCreate(savedInstanceState);
        setContentView(R.layout.activity_my);

        textView = (TextView) findViewById(R.id.text_view);
        editText = (EditText) findViewById(R.id.edit_text);
        Button helloButton = (Button) findViewById(R.id.hello_button);
        helloButton.setOnClickListener(new View.OnClickListener() {
            @Override
            public void onClick(View v) {
                sayHello(v);
            }
        });
    }

    public void sayHello(View view) {
        String name = editText.getText().toString();
        Intent intent = new Intent(this, WelcomeActivity.class);
        intent.putExtra("name", name);
        startActivity(intent);
    }
}
```

Robotium provides a class called `com.robotium.solo.Solo`, which wraps both the activity being tested and the `Instrumentation` object. It allows you to add text, click buttons, and more, without worrying about being on or off the UI thread. An example that tests the given activity is shown in Example 5-13.

Example 5-13. A Robotium test for MyActivity

```
public class MyActivityRobotiumTest
    extends ActivityInstrumentationTestCase2<MyActivity> {  ❶

    private Solo solo;  ❷

    public MyActivityRobotiumTest() {
        super(MyActivity.class);
    }

    public void setUp() {
        solo = new Solo(getInstrumentation(), getActivity());  ❸
    }

    public void testMyActivity() {
        solo.assertCurrentActivity("MyActivity", MyActivity.class);
    }

    public void testSayHello() {
        solo.enterText(0, "Dolly");
        solo.clickOnButton(
            getActivity().getString(R.string.hello_button_label));
        solo.assertCurrentActivity("WelcomeActivity", WelcomeActivity.class);
        solo.searchText("Hello, Dolly!");
    }

    public void tearDown() {
        solo.finishOpenedActivities();
    }
}
```

❶ Activity tests all extend this class

❷ The Solo reference from Robotium

❸ Instantiate the Solo reference

Robotium tests extend `ActivityInstrumentationTestCase2`, as with all activity tests. The `Solo` instance is initialized with the activity and retrieved instrumentation instances. The tests themselves use methods from the `Solo` class, like `enterText`, `clickOnButton`, or `searchText`.

The only downside to using Robotium is that the tests use the old JUnit 3 structure, with predefined `setUp` and `tearDown` methods as shown, and all tests have to follow the pattern `public void testXYZ()`. Still, the ease of writing the tests is remarkable.

The test class is stored in the same `androidTest` hierarchy as other Android tests, and executed on all emulators and connected devices simultaneously through the con nectedCheck task (Example 5-14).

Example 5-14. Executing the tests from Gradle

```
> ./gradlew connectedCheck
:app:preBuild UP-TO-DATE
:app:preDebugBuild UP-TO-DATE
:app:checkDebugManifest
:app:prepareDebugDependencies
// ... lots of tasks ...
:app:packageDebugAndroidTest UP-TO-DATE
:app:assembleDebugAndroidTest UP-TO-DATE
:app:connectedDebugAndroidTest
:app:connectedAndroidTest
:app:connectedCheck

BUILD SUCCESSFUL
```

The result is shown in Figure 5-9 after running on two emulators.

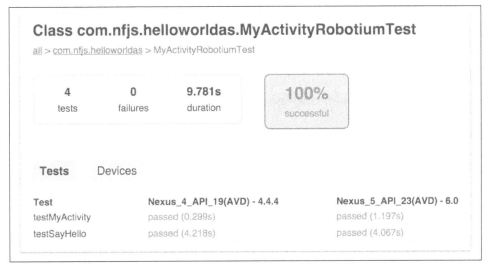

Figure 5-9. Robotium test output

Clicking the "Devices" button shows the same results, organized by device (Figure 5-10).

The full Robotium JavaDocs (*http://bit.ly/robotium-javadocs*) offer additional details and sample projects.

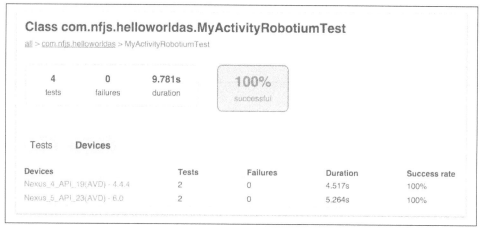

Class com.nfjs.helloworldas.MyActivityRobotiumTest

all > com.nfjs.helloworldas > MyActivityRobotiumTest

4	0	9.781s	100%
tests	failures	duration	successful

Tests   **Devices**

Devices	Tests	Failures	Duration	Success rate
Nexus_4_API_19(AVD) - 4.4.4	2	0	4.517s	100%
Nexus_5_API_23(AVD) - 6.0	2	0	5.264s	100%

Figure 5-10. Robotium test output organized by device

See Also

Activity testing using the Android Support Library is covered in Recipe 5.2. Testing with Espresso is covered in Recipe 5.4.

5.4 Activity Testing with Espresso

Problem

You want to test Android activities using the Espresso library from Google.

Solution

Add the Espresso dependencies to your Gradle build and write tests to use it.

Discussion

The Espresso testing library has been added to the "Android Test Kit" project, part of Google's testing tools for Android. Documentation for Espresso resides in a wiki (*http://bit.ly/espresso-docs*). Since Espresso is a Google project and specifically designed for Android, it's reasonable to assume that it will be the preferred mechanism for Android testing in the future.

While this is not a book on testing, setting up and running Espresso tests fits the normal Gradle practices, so a brief illustration is included here.

Espresso is included in the Android Support Repository, which is added under "Extras" in the SDK Manager. This process was illustrated in a figure in Recipe 5.2, repeated here in Figure 5-11.

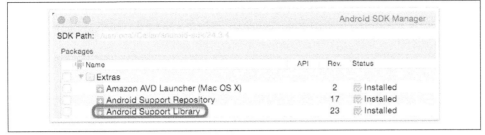

Figure 5-11. Adding the Android Support Library using the SDK Manager

To use Espresso in your project, add two `androidTestCompile` dependencies, as shown in Example 5-15.

Example 5-15. Adding the Espresso dependencies

```
dependencies {
    androidTestCompile 'com.android.support.test:runner:0.5'
    androidTestCompile 'com.android.support.test.espresso:espresso-core:2.2.2'
}
```

This actually leads to a conflict in versions of the support annotations library, because Espresso relies on version 23.1.1, while SDK 23 includes version 23.3.0 of the same library. You get an error similar to:

```
WARNING: Error:Conflict with dependency
'com.android.support:support-annotations'. Resolved versions for app (23.3.0) and
test app (23.1.1) differ. See http://g.co/androIDstudio/app-test-app-conflict
for details.
```

While that may be resolved by the time you build your application, let's make lemonade out of those lemons by showing how to fix it. In the top-level Gradle build file, simply force a resolution in the `allProjects` section, as shown in Example 5-16.

Example 5-16. Resolving a conflict in library versions

```
allprojects {
    repositories {
        jcenter()
    }

    configurations.all {
        resolutionStrategy.force
            'com.android.support:support-annotations:23.3.0'
    }
}
```

Espresso also requests that you set the `testInstrumentationRunner` in the `default`
`Config` block to use the `AndroidJUnitRunner`, as in Recipe 5.2. The complete module
build file therefore looks like that shown in Example 5-17.

Example 5-17. The full module build.gradle file

```
apply plugin: 'com.android.application'

android {
    compileSdkVersion 23
    buildToolsVersion "23.0.3"

    defaultConfig {
        applicationId "com.nfjs.helloworldas"
        minSdkVersion 16
        targetSdkVersion 23
        versionCode 1
        versionName "1.0"
        testInstrumentationRunner
            'android.support.test.runner.AndroidJUnitRunner'
    }
}

dependencies {
    compile 'com.android.support:support-annotations:23.3.0'
    androidTestCompile 'com.android.support.test:runner:0.5'
    androidTestCompile 'com.android.support.test.espresso:espresso-core:2.2.2'
}
```

Espresso tests love to use static methods, both in Espresso classes and in Hamcrest
matchers. Consequently, the test shown in Example 5-18 includes the import state-
ments for clarity.

Example 5-18. An Espresso test, with imports

```
package com.nfjs.helloworldas;

import android.support.test.rule.ActivityTestRule;
import android.support.test.runner.AndroidJUnit4;
import android.test.ActivityInstrumentationTestCase2;
import android.test.suitebuilder.annotation.MediumTest;

import org.junit.Rule;
import org.junit.Test;
import org.junit.runner.RunWith;

import static android.support.test.espresso.Espresso.onView;
import static android.support.test.espresso.action.ViewActions.click;
import static android.support.test.espresso.action.ViewActions.typeText;
import static android.support.test.espresso.assertion.ViewAssertions.matches;
```

```
import static android.support.test.espresso.matcher.ViewMatchers.withId;
import static android.support.test.espresso.matcher.ViewMatchers.withText;
import static org.hamcrest.CoreMatchers.containsString;

@RunWith(AndroidJUnit4.class)
@MediumTest
public class MyActivityEspressoTest
    extends ActivityInstrumentationTestCase2<MyActivity> {

    public MyActivityEspressoTest() {
        super(MyActivity.class);
    }

    @Rule
    public ActivityTestRule<MyActivity> mActivityRule =
        new ActivityTestRule<>(MyActivity.class);

    @Test
    public void testHelloWorld() {
        onView(withId(R.id.edit_text))
                .perform(typeText("Dolly"));
        onView(withId(R.id.hello_button))
                .perform(click());
        onView(withId(R.id.greeting_text))
                .check(matches(withText(containsString("Dolly"))));
    }
}
```

The simple DSL focuses on user actions rather than activities. From this test, it is not obvious that clicking the button actually shifted from the MyActivity class to the WelcomeActivity class, but that did in fact happen. The results are shown in Figure 5-12.

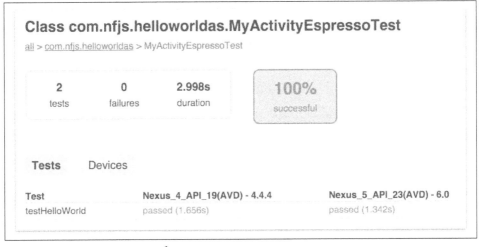

Figure 5-12. Espresso test results

Once again, clicking the "Devices" button shows the results organized by device rather than test, as in Figure 5-13.

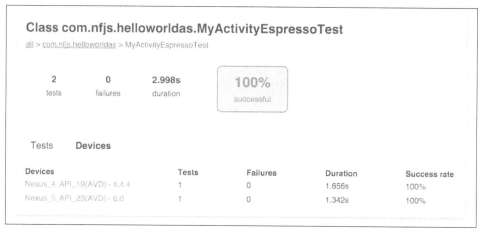

Figure 5-13. Espresso test results organized by device

Espresso is an interesting DSL approach to writing functional tests. It is likely to be a recommended API for the future.

Collecting Test Results

If your app includes multiple flavors or modules, the HTML test reports will be organized into separate subdirectories. This makes it tedious to examine each one individually.

Fortunately, there is a plug-in available to collect all the reports into a single build folder. In the top-level build file, after the `buildscript` block, include the `android-reporting` plug-in. See Example 5-19 for details.

Example 5-19. Adding the android-reporting plug-in

```
allprojects {
    repositories {
        jcenter()
    }

    configurations.all {
        resolutionStrategy.force
            'com.android.support:support-annotations:23.3.0'
    }
}

apply plugin: 'android-reporting' ❶
```

❶ The Android reporting plug-in collects test reports into a single file

Now if you run the `mergeAndroidReports` task, everything will be collected into a single file.

Example 5-20. Merging Android test reports

```
> ./gradlew deviceCheck mergeAndroidReports --continue
```

The `--continue` flag is a standard Gradle flag, telling the build to keep going even if there are failed tests. The result when running with multiple variants should be similar to that in Figure 5-14.

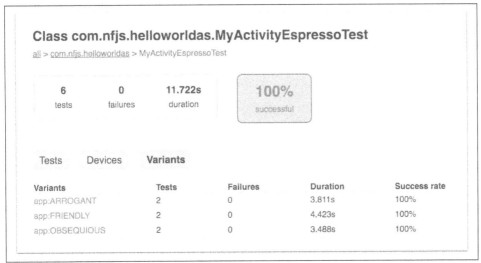

Figure 5-14. Merged test reports from app with multiple variants

See Also

Activity testing using the Android Support Library is covered in Recipe 5.2. Testing with the Robotium library is covered in Recipe 5.3. The technique listed here for merging test reports works with any tests, not just Espresso.

CHAPTER 6

Performance and Documentation

6.1 Performance Recommendations

Problem

You need to improve the performance of your Gradle build.

Solution

Use a combination of the techniques recommended here.

Discussion

First things first: these are *not* recommendations that will affect the performance of your app. There are many things you can do to help your app, many of which involve the ProGuard tool that comes with Android. This section is not about that—it's about improving the performance of the build itself.

This recipe discusses settings that can be added to the *gradle.properties* file in the root of the Android application. If you prefer to use global settings, add a file called *gradle.properties* to the *.gradle* subfolder in your home directory.

The Gradle daemon

The Gradle daemon is a background process that stays alive between builds, caching both data and code. Most recent versions of Gradle automatically start a Gradle daemon whenever you run from the command prompt.

By default, Android Studio starts a Gradle daemon in your project, with a timeout period of three hours, which is long enough for most development tasks. If you run

Gradle from the command line, however, you may not automatically start the daemon.

To make sure the daemon starts, add the setting shown in Example 6-1.

Example 6-1. Gradle daemon setting in gradle.properties

```
org.gradle.daemon=true
```

The daemon can also be started and stopped using a command-line flag. Use --daemon and --no-daemon to enable or disable the daemon on individual build invocations. Stopping it is sometimes useful if you're worried that the internal cache is out of date or if you're doing debugging. If you wish to stop a running daemon process, use the --stop argument to gradle.

 The Gradle team strongly recommends you do not use the daemon on continuous integration servers, which value stable and repeatable builds more than performance.

Parallel compilation

Gradle has an "incubating" option to compile independent projects in parallel. To use it, add a line to *gradle.properties*, as in Example 6-2.

Example 6-2. Parallel compilation setting in gradle.properties

```
org.gradle.parallel=true
```

Note that this may not help much. Most modules inside Android projects are related, which negates any benefit from parallel compilation.

Configuration on demand

Normally Gradle configures all tasks in all projects involved in a build before executing any of them. For projects with a large number of subprojects and many tasks, this can be inefficient. It is therefore possible to try to configure only the projects that are relevant for the requested tasks.

To do this, use the "configure on demand" setting in *gradle.properties*, as shown in Example 6-3.

Example 6-3. The configure on demand setting in gradle.properties

```
org.gradle.configureondemand=true
```

Most Android applications have only a small number of subprojects, so this feature may not be all that helpful.

Again, this is an incubating feature, so the specific details may change with new versions of Gradle.

Exclude unneeded tasks

As discussed in Recipe 4.3, the `-x` flag can be used to exclude a specific task, such as `lint`, that takes time but may not be needed during every build.

That recipe also shows how to disable particular tasks in the task graph after it has been assembled. See that recipe for details.

Change the JVM settings

Ultimately a Gradle build is running in a Java process, so flags that affect the JVM affect the performance of Gradle. Example 6-4 shows a handful of settings for the Java virtual machine.

Example 6-4. Choosing JVM setting in gradle.properties

```
org.gradle.jvmargs=-Xmx2048m -XX:MaxPermSize=512m
    -XX:+HeapDumpOnOutOfMemoryError
```

The `-Xmx` flag specifies the maximum amount of memory to use in the Java process. An `-Xms` flag specifies the initial amount of memory to allocate to the process. The example also changes the size of the "permanent generation" space, and dumps the heap to a file when a `java.lang.OutOfMemoryError` is thrown.

See the Java HotSpot VM options page for details.

Use only the dependencies you need

This specifically refers to Google Play services, which used to require a large library and now comes in the form of separate modules.

For example, to use Google Maps you used to have to add the entire Google Play services dependency at compile time, as in Example 6-5.

Example 6-5. Adding the entire Google Play services dependency

```
dependencies {
    compile 'com.google.android.gms:play-service:7.8.0'
}
```

This is a rather large library, with many dependencies. Figure 6-1 shows the list of added libraries once the full Google Play service dependency is added.

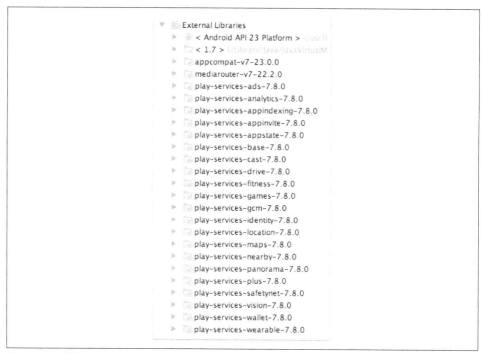

Figure 6-1. The complete set of Google Play services

With Android's 65K method name limitation, you would be adding a lot of method handles you don't need. Instead, add only the Maps dependency, as in Example 6-6.

Example 6-6. Adding the Google Maps dependency only

```
dependencies {
    compile 'com.google.android.gms:play-service-maps:7.8.0'
}
```

The contrast between the just the Maps service (as shown in Figure 6-2) is dramatic.

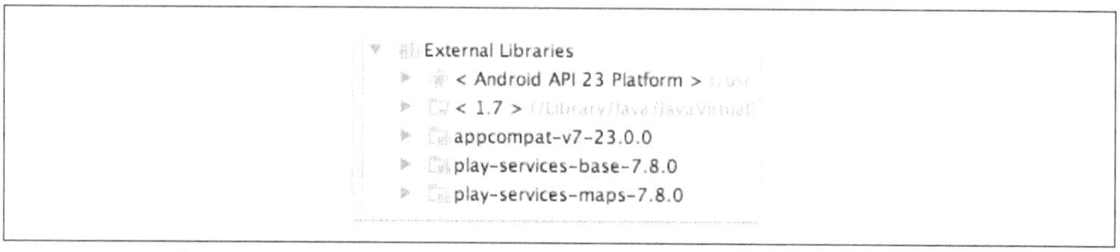

Figure 6-2. Adding the Google Maps dependency only

Use dex options

The Android block allows you specify options that control the "dex" process that converts Java byte codes (i.e., `.class` files) to Dalvik executables (`.dex` files). The `dexOptions` block contains the options in Example 6-7.

Example 6-7. The dexOptions block inside android

```
dexOptions {
    incremental true
    javaMaxHeapSize '2g'
    jumboMode = true
    preDexLibraries = true
}
```

The `incremental` option specifies whether to enable the incremental mode for the dx processor. As the documentation says, "this has many limitations and may not work. Use carefully."

Use `javaMaxHeapSize` as an alternative way of specifying `Xmx` values during the dx run, in 1024m increments—so here it is set to 2 gigs.

Enabling "jumbo mode" allows a larger number of strings in the dex files. If that's an issue, you may want to spend more time on configuring ProGuard.

The `preDexLibraries` will run the dx process on libraries ahead of time, just as it sounds. As the docs say, "this can improve incremental builds, but clean builds may be slower."

All of these settings can both help and hurt performance, so be sure to try them out before adopting them.

Profiling your build

You can run Gradle with the `--profile` command-line option to generate useful information about the build. The results will be written in HTML form to the *build/reports/profile* directory, this time in the top-level project.

As a sample, consider running the `assembleDebug` task from the multiflavor build described in Example 6-8.

Example 6-8. Running Gradle with the --profile option

```
> ./gradlew --profile assembleDebug
:app:preBuild UP-TO-DATE
:app:preArrogantStarkDebugBuild UP-TO-DATE
:app:checkArrogantStarkDebugManifest
:app:preArrogantStarkReleaseBuild UP-TO-DATE
:app:preArrogantWayneDebugBuild UP-TO-DATE
```

```
:app:preArrogantWayneReleaseBuild UP-TO-DATE
:app:preFriendlyStarkDebugBuild UP-TO-DATE
:app:preFriendlyStarkReleaseBuild UP-TO-DATE
:app:preFriendlyWayneDebugBuild UP-TO-DATE
:app:preFriendlyWayneReleaseBuild UP-TO-DATE
:app:preObsequiousStarkDebugBuild UP-TO-DATE
:app:preObsequiousStarkReleaseBuild UP-TO-DATE
:app:preObsequiousWayneDebugBuild UP-TO-DATE
:app:preObsequiousWayneReleaseBuild UP-TO-DATE
// ... tons of other tasks ...
:app:assembleObsequiousWayneDebug
:app:assembleDebug

BUILD SUCCESSFUL
```

The output report is in the *build/reports/profile* folder, with a filename of the form "profile-YYYY-MM-dd-hh-mm-ss.html", where the part after the word "profile" refers to timestamp quantities year, month, day, hour, minute, and seconds.

A sample report is shown in Figure 6-3.

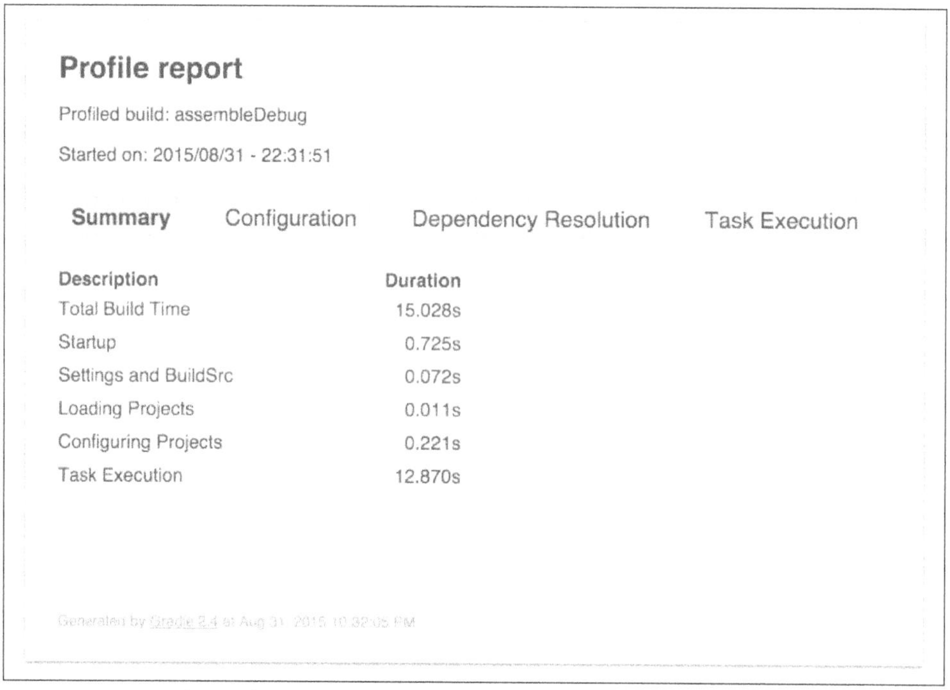

Profile report

Profiled build: assembleDebug

Started on: 2015/08/31 - 22:31:51

Summary	Configuration	Dependency Resolution	Task Execution

Description	Duration
Total Build Time	15.028s
Startup	0.725s
Settings and BuildSrc	0.072s
Loading Projects	0.011s
Configuring Projects	0.221s
Task Execution	12.870s

Generated by Gradle 2.4 at Aug 31, 2015, 10:32:05 PM

Figure 6-3. Sample profile report

The various tabs break down the summary report into individual configuration steps, configuration (which is minimal in this case), and execution. In a project this size there isn't a lot to see, but for larger projects this is a good way to find bottlenecks in your process.

See Also

The Java HotSpot VM options page for Java 7 and earlier is at *http://bit.ly/java-hotspot*. Recipe 4.3 shows how to exclude tasks from the assembled task graph.

6.2 DSL Documentation

Problem

You need to search the full documentation for the Android Gradle DSL.

Solution

Access the Gradle Tools website, and download a ZIP file from the Android Developer website.

Discussion

The home page for Android development (*http://developer.android.com*) holds the full API guides, JavaDoc references, tools documentation, and more. The contents there for the Android Gradle plug-in, however, are a bit thin.

Instead, the primary source for the Android plug-in to Gradle is hosted at the Android Tools Project Site (*http://bit.ly/as-new-build*), which contains the most recent information, as well as links to the Gradle Plugin User Guide (Figure 6-4).

The User Guide (*http://bit.ly/gradle-guide*) itself, shown in Figure 6-5, is useful, but often well out of date (which is one of the reasons this book exists).

Another link from the Android Tools Plugin Site is the DSL Reference (*http://bit.ly/github-gradle-dsl*), which takes you to a GitHub repository for the documentation (Figure 6-6). Fortunately, you don't need to clone the repository and build it to see the documentation. The front page (i.e., the *README.md* file, rendered automatically by GitHub) has a link to the most recent version (*http://bit.ly/gradle-dsl*).

The plug-in reference contains not just the DSL itself, with blocks like `buildTypes`, `productFlavors`, and `signingConfigs`, but also the actual types implementing them. For example, the `BuildType` page (part of the `com.android.build.gradle.internal.dsl` package) shows all properties and methods available in that class.

Figure 6-4. The Android Tools Project website

Figure 6-5. The Gradle Plugin User Guide

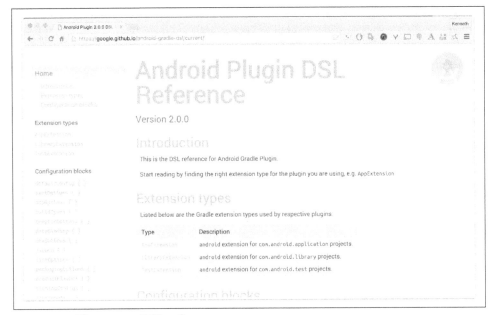

Figure 6-6. The current DSL reference

Finally, the Gradle website (*http://gradle.org*) contains links to the JavaDocs, Groovy-Docs, DSL reference, and the User Guide for Gradle (*http://bit.ly/gradle-user*) itself.

To summarize:

- Android Developer Site (*http://developer.android.com*)
- Android Tools Project (*http://bit.ly/android-tools-project*)
- Gradle Plugin User Guide (*http://bit.ly/grd-pl-guide*)
- DSL Reference (GitHub) (*http://github.com/google/android-gradle-dsl*)
- DSL Reference (rendered) (*http://bit.ly/gradle-pl-dsl*)
- Gradle User Guide (*http://bit.ly/gr-user-guide*)

Just Enough Groovy to Get By

This appendix reviews the basics of the Groovy programming language. The Gradle build files consist largely of a Domain Specific Language, written in Groovy, for builds. In addition to the DSL, any legal Groovy code can be added to the build.

Groovy is a general-purpose programming language, based on Java, that compiles to Java byte codes. While it has functional capabilities, it is an object-oriented language that is arguably the next-generation language in the path from C++ to Java.

Basic Syntax

The "Hello, World!" program for Groovy is the one-liner shown in Example A-1.

Example A-1. Hello, World! in Groovy

```
println 'Hello, World!'
```

Items of note:

- Semicolons are optional. If you add them, they work, but they're not required.
- Parentheses are optional until they're not. If the compiler guesses correctly where they should have gone, everything works. Otherwise, add them back in. The `println` method takes a `String` argument. Here the parentheses are left out.
- There are two types of strings in Groovy: single-quoted strings, like *Hello*, are instances of `java.lang.String`. Double-quoted strings are Groovy strings and allow interpolation, shown in Example A-2.

There are no "primitives" in Groovy. All variables use the wrapper classes, like `java.lang.Integer`, `java.lang.Character`, and `java.lang.Double`. The native data type for integer literals, like 3, is `Integer`. The native data type for floating point literals, like 3.5, is `java.math.BigDecimal`.

Example A-2. Some basic data types in Groovy

```
assert 3.class == Integer
assert (3.5).class == BigDecimal
assert 'abc' instanceof String   ❶
assert "abc" instanceof String   ❷

String name = 'Dolly'
assert "Hello, ${name}!" == 'Hello, Dolly!'   ❸
assert "Hello, $name!" == 'Hello, Dolly!'   ❹
assert "Hello, $name!" instanceof GString
```

❶ Single-quoted strings are Java strings

❷ Double-quoted strings are also Java strings unless you interpolate

❸ String interpolation, full form

❹ String interpolation, short form when there is no ambiguity

Note that you can invoke methods on literals, because they are instances of the wrapper classes.

Groovy lets you declare variables with either an actual type, like `String`, `Date`, or `Employee`, or you can use `def`. See Example A-3.

Example A-3. Static versus dynamic data types

```
Integer n = 3
Date now = new Date()

def x = 3
assert x.class == Integer
x = 'abc'
assert x.class == String
x = new Date()
assert x.class == Date
```

Java imports the `java.lang` package automatically. In Groovy, the following packages are all automatically imported:

- `java.lang`
- `java.util`
- `java.io`

- `java.net`
- `groovy.lang`
- `groovy.util`

The classes `java.math.BigInteger` and `java.math.BigDecimal` are also available without an import statement.

The assert Method and the Groovy Truth

The `assert` method in Groovy evaluates its argument according to the "Groovy Truth." That means:

- Nonzero numbers (positive and negative) are true
- Nonempty collections, including strings, are true
- Nonnull references are true
- Boolean `true` is true

The Groovy Truth is illustrated in Example A-4.

Example A-4. The Groovy Truth

```
assert 3;     assert -1;  assert !0
assert 'abc'; assert !''; assert !""

assert [3, 1, 4, 1, 5, 9]
assert ![]
```

Asserts that pass return nothing. Asserts that fail throw an exception, as in Example A-5, with lots of debugging information included.

Example A-5. Failing assertions

```
int x = 5; int y = 7
assert 12 == x + y  // passes

assert 12 == 3 * x + 4.5 * y / (2/x + y**3)  // fails
```

The result of the failing assertion is shown in Example A-6.

Example A-6. Failing assert output

```
Exception thrown

Assertion failed:
```

```
assert 12 == 3 * x + 4.5 * y / (2/x + y**3)
           |   | | |     | | |   || | ||
       false| 5 |     | 7 |   |5 | |343
          15 |       31.5|   0.4| 7
             |           |       343.4
             |         0.0917297612
          15.0917297612
```

```
      at ConsoleScript11.run(ConsoleScript11:4)
```

Operator Overloading

In Groovy, every operator corresponds to a method call. For example, the + sign invokes the plus method on Number. This is used extensively in the Groovy libraries. Some examples are shown in Example A-7.

Example A-7. Operator overloading

```
assert 3 + 4 == 3.plus(4)
assert 3 * 4 == 3.multiply(4)

assert 2**6 == 64
assert 2**6 == 2.power(6)

assert 'abc' * 3 == 'abcabcabc' // String.multiply(Number)
try {
    3 * 'abc'
} catch (MissingMethodException e) {
    // no Number.multiply(String) method
}

String s = 'this is a string'
assert s + ' and more' == 'this is a string and more'
assert s - 'is' == 'th is a string'
assert s - 'is' - 'is' == 'th  a string'

Date now = new Date()
Date tomorrow = now + 1 // Date.plus(Integer)
assert tomorrow - 1 == now  // Date.minus(Integer)
```

Groovy has an exponentiation operator, **, as shown.

In Java, the == operator checks that two references are assigned to the same object. In Groovy, == invokes the equals method, so it checks for equivalence rather than equality. If you want to check references, use the is method.

Collections

Groovy has native syntax for collections. Use square brackets and separate values by commas to create an `ArrayList`. You can use the `as` operator to convert one collection type to another. Collections also have operator overloading, implementing methods like `plus`, `minus`, and `multiply` (Example A-8).

Example A-8. Collection examples and methods

```
def nums = [3, 1, 4, 1, 5, 9, 2, 6, 5]
assert nums instanceof ArrayList

Set uniques = nums as Set
assert uniques == [3, 1, 4, 5, 9, 2, 6] as Set

def sorted = nums as SortedSet
assert sorted == [1, 2, 3, 4, 5, 6, 9] as SortedSet
assert sorted instanceof TreeSet

assert nums[0] == 3
assert nums[1] == 1
assert nums[-1] == 5 // end of list
assert nums[-2] == 6

assert nums[0..3] == [3, 1, 4, 1]  // two dots is a Range
assert nums[-3..-1] == [2, 6, 5]
assert nums[-1..-3] == [5, 6, 2]

String hello = 'hello'
assert 'olleh' == hello[-1..0]  // Strings are collections too
```

A Range in Groovy consists of two values separated by a pair of dots, as in `from..to`. The range expands starting at the `from` position, invoking `next` on each element until it reaches the `to` position, inclusive.

Maps use a colon notation to separate the keys from the values. The square bracket operator on a map is the `getAt` or `putAt` method, depending on whether you are accessing or adding a value. The dot operator is overloaded similarly. See Example A-9 for details.

Example A-9. Map instances and methods

```
def map = [a:1, b:2, c:2]
assert map.getClass() == LinkedHashMap
assert map.a == 1  ❶
assert map['b'] == 2 ❷
assert map.get('c') == 2  ❸
```

❶ Overloaded dot is put here

❷ Uses putAt method

❸ Java still works, too

Closures

Groovy has a class called Closure that represents a block of code that can be used like an object. Think of it as the body of an anonymous method, which is an oversimplification but not a bad start.

A closure is like a Java 8 lambda, in that it takes arguments and evaluates a block of code. Groovy closures can modify variables defined outside them, however, and Java 8 does not have a class called Lambda.

Many methods in Groovy take closures as arguments. For example, the each method on collections supplies each element to a closure, which is evaluated with it. An example is in Example A-10.

Example A-10. Using Groovy's each method with a closure argument

```
def nums = [3, 1, 4, 1, 5, 9]

def doubles = []  ❶
nums.each { n ->  ❷
    doubles << n * 2  ❸
}

assert doubles == [6, 2, 8, 2, 10, 18]
```

❶ Empty list

❷ each takes a closure of one argument, before the arrow, here called n

❸ Left-shift operator appends to a collection

> Modifying a variable defined outside a closure is considered a side-effect, and not good practice. The collect method, discussed later, is preferred.

This is a natural way to double the values in a list, but there is a better alternative, called collect. The collect method transforms a collection into a new one by applying a closure to each element. It is similar to the map method from Java 8, or just think of it as the map operation in a map-filter-reduce process (Example A-11).

Example A-11. Using Groovy's collect method to transform a collection

```
def nums = [3, 1, 4, 1, 5, 9]
def doubles == nums.collect { it * 2 }
assert doubles == [6, 2, 8, 2, 10, 18]
```

When a closure has a single argument (which is the default), and you don't give that argument a name using the arrow operator, the dummy name defaults to the word it. In this case, the collect method creates the doubles collection by applying it * 2 in a closure to each element.

POGOs

Java classes with just attributes and getters and setters are often called Plain Old Java Objects, or POJOs. Groovy has similar classes called POGOs. An example is in Example A-12.

Example A-12. A simple POGO

```
import groovy.transform.Canonical
@Canonical
class Event {
    String name
    Date when
    int priority
}
```

This little class actually has a lot of power. For a POGO:

- The class is public by default
- Attributes are private by default
- Methods are public by default
- Getter and setter methods are generated for each attribute not marked public or private
- Both a default constructor and a "map-based" constructor (uses arguments of the form "attribute:value") are provided

In addition, this POGO include the @Canonical annotation, which triggers an Abstract Syntax Tree (AST) transformation. AST transformations modify the syntax tree created by the compiler during the compilation process in specific ways.

The @Canonical annotation is actually a shortcut for three other AST transformations: @ToString, @EqualsAndHashCode, and @TupleConstructor. Each does what they sound like, so in this case, the @Canonical annotation adds to this class:

- A toString override that displays the fully-qualified name of the class, followed by the values of the attributes, in order from top down
- An equals override that does a null-safe check for equivalence on each attribute
- A hashCode override that generates an integer based on the values of the attributes in a fashion similar to that laid out by Joshua Bloch in his *Effective Java* (Addison-Wesley) book long ago
- An additional constructor that takes the attributes as arguments, in order

That's a lot of productivity for seven lines of code. Example A-13 shows how to use it.

Example A-13. Using the Event POGO

```
Event e1 = new Event(name: 'Android Studio 1.0',
    when: Date.parse('MMM dd, yyyy', 'Dec 8, 2014'),
    priority: 1)

Event e2 = new Event(name: 'Android Studio 1.0',
    when: Date.parse('MMM dd, yyyy', 'Dec 8, 2014'),
    priority: 1)

assert e1.toString() ==
    'Event(Android Studio 1.0, Mon Dec 08 00:00:00 EST 2014, 1)'
assert e1 == e2

Set events = [e1, e2]
assert events.size() == 1
```

Gradle uses all these features, and more, but this summary should get you started.

Groovy in Gradle Build Files

Gradle build files support all Groovy syntax. Here are few specific examples, however, that illustrate Groovy in Gradle.

In Example A-14, the word apply is a method on the Project instance. The parentheses on the method are optional, and left out here. The argument is setting a property called plugin on the Project instance to the string value supplied.

Example A-14. Applying the Android plugin for Gradle

```
apply plugin: 'com.android.application'
```

In Example A-15, the term android is part of the plug-in's DSL, which takes a closure as an argument. Properties inside the closure, like compileSdkVersion, are method calls with optional parentheses. In some Gradle build files, properties are assigned using =, which would invoke a corresponding setter method. The developers of the Android plug-in frequently added a regular method, like compileSdkVersion(23), in addition to the setter, setCompileSdkVersion(23).

Example A-15. Setting properties in the android block

```
android {
    compileSdkVersion 23
    buildToolsVersion "23.0.1"
}
```

Also, "nested" properties, like compileSdkVersion here, can be set using a dot notation as an alternative:

```
    android.compileSdkVersion = 23
```

Both are equivalent.

Recent versions of the plug-in add a clean task to the Gradle build file. This task has name called clean, is an instance of the Delete class (as subclass of Task), and takes a closure as an argument. In keeping with standard Groovy practice, the closure is shown after the parentheses (Example A-16).

Example A-16. The default clean task

```
task clean(type: Delete) {
    delete rootProject.buildDir
}
```

> If a Groovy method takes a Closure as its last argument, the closure is normally added after the parentheses.

The implementation here invokes the delete method (again, with optional parentheses) on the rootProject.buildDir. The value of the rootProject property is the top-level project, and the default value of buildDir is "build," so this task deletes the "build" directory in the top-level project.

Note that calling clean in the top-level project will also invoke it on the app subproject, which will delete the *build* directory there as well.

In Example A-17, the `compile` term is part of the DSL, implying that its argument is applied during the `compile` phase. The `fileTree` method is shown with parentheses, though they could be left out. The `dir` argument takes a string representing a local directory. The `include` argument takes a Groovy list (the square brackets) of file patterns.

Example A-17. A file tree dependency

```
dependencies {
    compile fileTree(dir: 'libs', include: ['*.jar'])
}
```

See Also

The book *Making Java Groovy* (*http://bit.ly/java-groovy*), by Ken Kousen (Manning), discusses Groovy and integrates it with Java, and also has a chapter on build processes with Gradle. The definitive reference for Groovy is *Groovy in Action* (*http://bit.ly/groovy-action-2e*), Second Edition, by Dierk Konig, Paul King, et al. (Manning).

The Groovy home page is at *http://groovy-lang.org*, and contains extensive documentation.

O'Reilly also has three video courses on Groovy: *Groovy Programming Fundamentals* (*http://bit.ly/groovy-programming-fundamentals*), *Practical Groovy Programming* (*http://bit.ly/practical-groovy-programming*), and *Mastering Groovy Programming* (*http://bit.ly/mastering-groovy-programming*). All three are available on Safari (*http://www.safaribooksonline.com*) as well.

Gradle Basics

The recipes in this book are for the Gradle build files inside of Android. Gradle is a powerful build tool, however, which is used extensively in other projects. This appendix reviews the basics of Gradle. All capabilities reviewed here can be used inside Android build files as well.

Installing Gradle

 You do not need to install Gradle to use it in Android projects. Android Studio includes Gradle, and provides a Gradle wrapper as well. Its use is demonstrated in Recipe 4.1, among other recipes.

Gradle comes as a single, ZIP download. You merely need to download the latest distribution from the Gradle website (*http://gradle.org*) to get started. Installation is as easy as:

1. Download and unzip the distribution

2. Set a GRADLE_HOME environment variable to point to the unzipped folder

3. Add the *bin* folder under GRADLE_HOME to your path

The gradle command can then be executed at the root of any project. By default the build file is called *build.gradle*, but any name can be used. The -b or --build-file flag is used to specify a different build file.

As an alternative, Gradle provides a *wrapper*, which can be used to automatically download and install Gradle on its first use. The wrapper is demonstrated later in this appendix.

Note that though Gradle build files are written in Groovy, you don't need to install Groovy to run Gradle. Gradle includes a distribution of Groovy inside it, which is used to power the build.

To see the details of the Gradle installation, run Gradle with the -v flag, as shown in Example B-1.

Example B-1. Displaying the Gradle version

```
> gradle -v

------------------------------------------------------------
Gradle 2.12
------------------------------------------------------------

Build time:   2016-03-14 08:32:03 UTC
Build number: none
Revision:     b29fbb64ad6b068cb3f05f7e40dc670472129bc0

Groovy:       2.4.4
Ant:          Apache Ant(TM) version 1.9.3 compiled on December 23 2013
JVM:          1.8.0 (Oracle Corporation 25.0-b70)
OS:           Mac OS X 10.11.4 x86_64
```

The Gradle version here is 2.12, which includes Groovy 2.4.4 under the hood, and is running on Java 1.8 on Mac OS X machine.

Build Lifecycle

Gradle builds run through three distinct phases:

Initialization
> Read environment configuration files *init.gradle* and *gradle.properties*, and set up all subprojects listed in_settings.gradle_

Configuration
> Evaluate all build scripts and build the model, including the DAG

Execution
> Execute the desired tasks

Java Projects

Gradle build files consist of *tasks*, which are assembled into a DAG. Custom tasks are discussed in the next section. Gradle is a plugin-based architecture, however, and by adding plugins to a build, you add tasks and capabilities to the build.

The most common plugin used outside the Android world is the Java plugin. Since this plugin comes with the Gradle distribution, adding it to your project is a simple as using the `apply` command. An example is shown in Example B-2.

Example B-2. A minimal build.gradle file for a Java project

```
apply plugin: 'java'
```

In fact, this is a complete build file for a Java project. The plugin itself defines a series of related tasks. To see what tasks are available, go to a command prompt in the root of the project and execute the `tasks` command. Sample output is shown in Example B-3.

Example B-3. Sample output from the tasks command

```
> gradle tasks
:tasks

------------------------------------------------------------
All tasks runnable from root project
------------------------------------------------------------

Build Setup tasks
-----------------
init - Initializes a new Gradle build. [incubating]
wrapper - Generates Gradle wrapper files. [incubating]

Help tasks
----------
components - Displays the components produced by root project 'gradle'. [incubating]
dependencies - Displays all dependencies declared in root project 'gradle'.
dependencyInsight - Displays the insight into a specific dependency in 'gradle'.
help - Displays a help message.
model - Displays the configuration model of root project 'gradle'. [incubating]
projects - Displays the sub-projects of root project 'gradle'.
properties - Displays the properties of root project 'gradle'.
tasks - Displays the tasks runnable from root project 'gradle'.
```

The list of tasks shows which are available, but does not show their relationships. Additional command-line flags are available for that, but the easiest way to see what tasks are run in which order is simply to execute the `build` task. Executing a build is shown in Example B-4.

Example B-4. Executing a Gradle build

```
> gradle build
:compileJava UP-TO-DATE
:processResources UP-TO-DATE
```

```
:classes UP-TO-DATE
:jar
:assemble
:compileTestJava UP-TO-DATE
:processTestResources UP-TO-DATE
:testClasses UP-TO-DATE
:test UP-TO-DATE
:check UP-TO-DATE
:build

BUILD SUCCESSFUL

Total time: 1.956 secs
```

Each phase, like :build, depends on others. The plugin defines the tasks and their relationships. Gradle then executes them in the proper order.

The tasks form a directed acyclic graph. In this case, the graph showing the relationships is available in the Gradle User Guide (*http://bit.ly/gradle-java*). Figure B-1, taken from the online documentation, shows the DAG for the Java plugin.

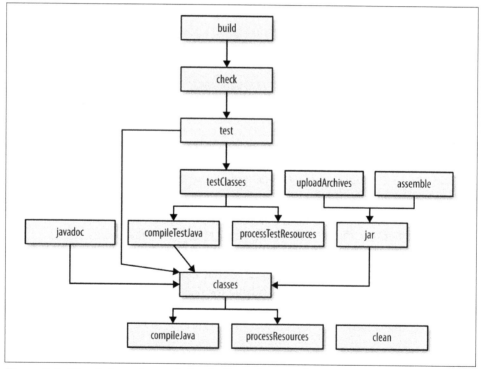

Figure B-1. Directed acyclic graph for the Java plugin tasks

Each association uses an arrow (which is the *directed* part), and while there are multiple relationships, there are no loops in the graph (thus the *acyclic* label). Running the `build` task means that first the `check` and `assemble` tasks must be run. The `check` task then depends on `test`, which depends on `testClasses` and `classes`, and so on.

The Java plugin assumes that the source code is laid out in a directory structure first standardized by Maven. Nontesting code is placed in an *src/main/java* folder, and tests go in *src/main/test* by default. This is easy enough to customize through *source sets*.

From the Gradle point of view, Android projects are *not* Java projects. They use a different plugin and (slightly) different project layout.

Repositories and Dependencies

The current build file defines testing tasks, but not a testing library. The build file from Example B-5 is far more typical of basic Java projects.

Example B-5. A Gradle build with a repository and dependencies

```
apply plugin: 'java'

repositories {
    jcenter()
}

dependencies {
    testCompile 'junit:junit:4.12'
}
```

Gradle defines a Domain Specific Language (DSL) for builds. The `repositories` and `dependencies` elements in the build file are part of the DSL.

Repositories are collections of libraries that can be retrieved on demand and stored in a local cache, which defaults to a *.gradle* folder in the user's home directory. The repository used in this build file is called `jcenter()`, which is the Bintray JCenter Artifactory repository. Another built-in repository is `mavenCentral()`, the public Maven Central Repository. Multiple repositories are frequently included in a build file. Each is searched in turn to resolve dependencies.

Dependencies are listed, naturally enough, in the `dependencies` block. A dependency includes both the information about the library (group, name, and version), as well as the "dependency configuration" where it is needed.

The predefined dependency configurations for the Java plugin are:

- compile
- runtime
- testCompile
- testRuntime
- archives
- default

The first four are the most common, but all mean pretty much what they sound like. For example, a compile dependency makes the library classes available throughout the project, which a testCompile dependency adds the library classes only to the *src/test/java* source tree. JDBC drivers are often listed as runtime dependencies, or even testRuntime dependencies if the database is only used for testing.

Custom Tasks

The Gradle DSL is extensive, and often you won't need anything beyond what the plugins provide. Sooner or later, however, every build becomes a custom build, and Gradle was designed with that in mind.

Recipe 4.1 discusses how to create your own tasks for Gradle builds.

Use the task keyword to define a task, as in Example B-6.

Example B-6. Custom task to say hello

```
def task {
    doLast {
        println 'hello'
    }
}
```

The doLast block indicates code that should be run at *execution* time. Any code outside that block (but still inside the task) is run at *configuration* time.

Gradle also includes a doFirst block, but it is used far less often. Also, you can abbreviate the doLast block using a left-shift operator.

The entire task in Example B-7 is run at execution time. It's easy enough to overlook the syntax, however, which is one of the reasons this approach is not preferred.

Example B-7. Custom task using left-shift operator

```
def task << {
    println 'hello'
}
```

The Gradle API has many built-in tasks available, which can be customized. For example, Example B-8 configures the Copy task, which is a class in the Gradle API.

Example B-8. Configuring the Copy task

```
def copyOutputs(type: Copy) {
    from "$buildDir/outputs/apk"
    into '../results'
}
```

Gradle files often mix single-quoted and double-quoted strings. Double-quoted strings allow interpolation, and single-quoted strings don't. Otherwise they are effectively identical.

The Copy task itself includes both configuration and execution time sections. In this case, setting the from and into properties assigns the desired values, and the task handles the rest. This approach to configuring existing tasks rather than writing your own is considered a good practice, because it favors telling Gradle what you would like rather than specifying how to do it.

Multiproject Builds

Subdirectories of a given project can be Gradle projects themselves, with their own build files and dependencies. In fact, they can even depend on each other.

The file *settings.gradle* specifies which subdirectories are Gradle projects. In a typical Android app, *settings.gradle* includes the *app* directory, which is where the code for the actual application resides.

Each app in a multiproject build can have its own build file. To share common blocks among projects, use a subprojects or an allprojects block, both of which configure the overall instance of the Project class. Details of this process are discussed in Recipe 1.1.

In fact, the rest of this book discusses how Gradle works with Android projects, which is as good a place as any to end this appendix.

See Also

The home page for Gradle (*http://gradle.org*) contains extensive documentation. O'Reilly also has books on Gradle: *Building and Testing with Gradle* by Tim Berglund and Matthew McCullogh, and *Gradle Beyond the Basics* by Tim Berglund, are in the same series as this book.

Two video courses are available from O'Reilly as well: *Gradle Fundamentals*, and *Gradle for Android*. Both are on Safari (*https://www.safaribooksonline.com*).

Index

Symbols

@ (at sign), in dependency notation, 23
" " (double quotes), enclosing strings, 18, 129
<< (left-shift operator), for doLast block, 144-145
() (parentheses), in Groovy, 129
; (semicolon), in Groovy, 129
' ' (single quotes), enclosing strings, 18, 129
*. (spread-dot operator), 84
[] (square brackets), for collections, 133

A

aar files, 88
    (see also Android libraries)
activities
    functional testing for, 108-117
    for specific flavors, 71-75
ADP timeout period, extending, 80
ADT plug-in for Eclipse, 37-39
allprojects block, 5, 43-45
allTasks property, 84
android block, 6, 7-8
Android Gradle DSL documentation, 125-127
Android libraries
    adding to applications, 88-96
    libraryVariants property for, 78
    as subprojects, 44
Android package (APK), signing, 45-51
Android plug-in for Gradle, 5-7, 136
android property, 78
Android SDK
    configuring, 6
    Robolectric as mock of, 102
    versions of, ix, 6-9

Android Studio
    adding dependencies, 23-25
    building projects, 15-17
    building specific variants, 59
    configuring applications, 8
    creating Android libraries, 89-91
    creating projects, 2-4
    importing Eclipse ADT projects, 33-37
    signing an APK, 49-51
    synchronizing projects, 20
    unit testing, for Java components, 97-103
    versions of, ix
Android Support Repository, 103, 112
Android Testing Support Library, 103-107
Android versions, ix
android-reporting plug-in, 116-117
AndroidJUnitRunner class, 104, 106
AndroidManifest.xml file, 37
anonymous inner class, 44
APK (Android package), signing, 45-51
applicationId property, 8, 54-57
applicationIDsuffix property, 54-56
applications, 1
    (see also projects)
    Android library dependencies, adding, 88-96
    building (see build files; builds)
    configuring, 6-9
    Java library dependencies, adding, 18-25
    projects for, creating, 2-4
    testing (see testing)
applicationVariants property, 78
apply command, 6, 136, 141
assemble task, 59

assert method, 131-131
at sign (@), in dependency notation, 23

B

build files, 1-6, 15, 136-138, 140
build task, 11-13
build types, 53-56, 59
    (see also variants)
build.gradle file
    at app level, 5-6
    at top level, 4-5, 7-8
    synchronizing after editing, 20
builds
    adding custom tasks to, 80-82
    applicationIds for, 8, 54-57
    excluding tasks from, 83-84, 121
    executing in Android Studio, 15
    executing on command line, 9-15, 141
    lifecycle of, 140
    multiple, on one device (see build types; fla-
        vors; variants)
    multiproject builds, 145
    parallel compilation for, 120
    performance of, improving, 119-125
    profiling, 123-125
buildscript block, 5
buildToolsVersion property, 7, 8
BuildType class, 54
buildTypes block, 53-56

C

@Canonical annotation, 135
classes, for specific flavors, 71-75
clean task, 137
closures, in Groovy, 44, 134-135
code examples in this book, xi
collections, in Groovy, 133
com.android.application file (see Android plug-
    in for Gradle)
compilation, parallel, 120
compileoptions block, 8
compileSdkVersion property, 7
configuration on demand, 120
configuration phase, 78, 140
configurations, for dependencies, 18, 144
configuring applications, 6-9
configuring repositories, 26-28
connectedCheck task, 106
Copy task, customizing, 77-78

D

DAG (directed acyclic graph), 5, 140, 142
    adding custom tasks to, 80-82
    built in configuration phase, 78
data types, in Groovy, 130
debug build type, 53
debug keystore, 45
debuggable property, 54
def keyword, 30
defaultConfig block, 8
dependencies, 143-144
    Android, adding to applications, 88-96
    Java, adding to applications, 18-25
    limiting number of, 121-122
    resolving, repositories for, 26-28
    transitive, 21-23
    version numbers in, 18
dependencies block, 6, 18-25, 88-96
dependsOn method, 79
dependsOn property, 80-82
dexOptions block, 123
directed acyclic graph (see DAG)
distributionUrl property, 10
documentation for Android Gradle DSL,
    125-127
doFirst block, 144
doLast block, 78, 144-145
double quotes (" "), enclosing strings, 18, 129
DSL (Domain Specific Language), 6, 143
    (see also specific blocks)
DSL documentation, 125-127

E

Eclipse ADT projects
    exporting using ADT plug-in, 37-39
    importing into Android Studio, 33-37
Espresso library, 112-117
execution phase, 78, 140
ext block, 29-32

F

files (see build files; resources; source sets)
flavors, 56-59
    (see also variants)
    building, 59
    dimensions of, 67-70
    Java sources specific to, 71-75
functional interfaces, 45

Z

zipStoreBase property, 10

zipStorePath property, 10

About the Author

Ken Kousen is an independent consultant and trainer specializing in Android, Spring, Hibernate, Groovy, Grails, and Gradle. He holds numerous technical certifications, along with BS degrees in both Mathematics, and Mechanical and Aerospace Engineering from M.I.T., an MA and a PhD in Aerospace Engineering from Princeton, and an MS in Computer Science from R.P.I.

Colophon

The animal on the cover of *Gradle Recipes for Android* is a great potoo (*Nyctibius grandis*). This unusual creature occupies humid forest habitats throughout Central and South America.

The great potoo is a large bird at 18 to 24 inches long, with an average wingspan of 29 inches. It is somewhat owl-like in appearance, possessing a large head, a wide, gaping mouth, and immense yellow eyes. Its plumage is mottled light brown and gray, serving as camouflage against tree bark. The great potoo perches on branches, where it rests during the day and waits to capture prey at night; its diet includes large, flying insects as well as the occasional bat.

Solitary and elusive, little is known about the breeding habits of *Nyctibius grandis*. It lays just one egg per year, not in nests but in the notches of tree branches at least 30 feet above the ground.

The great potoo makes deep, guttural calls throughout the night. The haunting, unique sound has lent itself to many folk legends about the bird; some believe its plaintive cry is that of a shaman's daughter mourning her lost love, while others imagine the bird's song summons messages from the dead.

Many of the animals on O'Reilly covers are endangered; all of them are important to the world. To learn more about how you can help, go to *animals.oreilly.com*.

The cover image is from *Lydekker's Royal Natural History, Volume 4* and *Dover Pictorial Archive*. The cover fonts are URW Typewriter and Guardian Sans. The text font is Adobe Minion Pro; the heading font is Adobe Myriad Condensed; and the code font is Dalton Maag's Ubuntu Mono.

Get even more for your money.

Join the O'Reilly Community, and register the O'Reilly books you own. It's free, and you'll get:

- $4.99 ebook upgrade offer
- 40% upgrade offer on O'Reilly print books
- Membership discounts on books and events
- Free lifetime updates to ebooks and videos
- Multiple ebook formats, DRM FREE
- Participation in the O'Reilly community
- Newsletters
- Account management
- 100% Satisfaction Guarantee

Signing up is easy:

1. Go to: oreilly.com/go/register
2. Create an O'Reilly login.
3. Provide your address.
4. Register your books.

Note: English-language books only

To order books online:
oreilly.com/store

For questions about products or an order:
orders@oreilly.com

To sign up to get topic-specific email announcements and/or news about upcoming books, conferences, special offers, and new technologies:
elists@oreilly.com

For technical questions about book content:
booktech@oreilly.com

To submit new book proposals to our editors:
proposals@oreilly.com

O'Reilly books are available in multiple DRM-free ebook formats. For more information:
oreilly.com/ebooks

O'REILLY®

©2014 O'Reilly Media, Inc. O'Reilly logo is a registered trademark of O'Reilly Media, Inc. 14373

Ingram Content Group UK Ltd.
Milton Keynes UK
UKHW031821130323
418508UK00010B/960